The Race

From Pit Row to Victory Lane

R I C K   L E M O N S

WINEPRESS WP PUBLISHING

WinePress Publishing (PO Box 428, Enumclaw, WA 98022) functions only as book publisher. As such, the ultimate design, content, editorial accuracy, and views expressed or implied in this work are those of the author.

Unless otherwise noted, all Scriptures are taken from the *Holy Bible, New International Version*®, *NIV*®. Copyright © 1973, 1978, 1984 by the International Bible Society. Used by permission of Zondervan. All rights reserved.

Scripture references marked ASV are taken from the *Holy Bible, American Standard Version,* copyright © 1901, public domain.

Scripture references marked KJV are taken from the *King James Version* of the Bible.

Song lyrics from "Here I Am to Worship Light of the World," written by Tim Hughes, © 2001 Thankyou Music (admin. by EMI Christian Music Publishing c/o:Music Services). All Rights Reserved. Used By Permission.

ISBN 13: 978-1-57921-962-8
ISBN 10: 1-57921-962-4
Library of Congress Catalog Card Number: 2008923607

To my wonderful parents,
J.T. and Aunita Lemons

Thank you for your perseverance in the race and
your faithful devotion to the Lord Jesus Christ.
Thank you for your example to your family and
for helping all of us in the race
that God has marked out for us. Your lives have influenced us, and
your help and guidance have been my inspiration.
May your faithfulness to and love
for the Lord be known by all who read this book.

And in memory of my father-in-law,
James Barnett,
Who completed his race on August 11, 2005.
A big man! A big heart! A big smile! A man called Slim.
A devoted husband, Papa, and Papaw. Faithful friend.
He waits for us in heaven's Victory Lane.

CONTENTS

Foreword

Most American teenagers grow up hankering to fulfill a dream of driving a sports car as fast as the car will go. While American highways have always had speed limits, and my parents drummed into my head the importance of honoring the laws of the land, I still dreamed of an opportunity to drive someplace where there wasn't *any* speed limit. Consequently, when I made my first trip to Germany, I could not wait to get on the Autobahn. There, no speed limits exist and some very precise rules of driving etiquette limit the number of accidents that occur, despite average speeds of well over 120 miles an hour.

I have also been to Egypt. There I saw the Sphinx, a massive bedrock carving that stares straightforward and never moves. When I glanced to my right as I was negotiating a right-hand curve on the Autobahn somewhere between Vienna, Austria, and Brussels, Belgium, I saw my wife in the passenger seat, looking exactly like the Sphinx, unmoving and staring straight ahead. She was terrified, and I was having the time of my life. I was driving at about 130 miles an hour at that point and fulfilling a dream of high adventure.

In America, the only people who get to do that sort of thing, at least legally, are those who become NASCAR drivers. They are the envy of America, as demonstrated by the hundreds of thousands of people who sit at the racetrack every weekend watching the cars make endless revolutions around the track. You can be certain that almost every man in the stands would give his right arm to be driving. Alas, for most of us there is little chance that we will ever be a part of that adventure.

Wait a minute. As it turns out, while the adventure may be a little different, a high-risk experience, with the promise of incredible reward, at speeds faster than any of us can ever really imagine, *is* available to every single individual, at least according to Rick Lemons. In this book,

The Race—From Pit Row to Victory Lane, the pastor of the Fellowship Baptist Church in Forney, Texas has made the appropriate observation that life's adventure can be more compelling than any NASCAR race-track. As a matter of fact, Lemons, who has long been a keen observer of NASCAR, has noted that life resembles a NASCAR race in more ways than most of us have ever imagined. In this book, he captures those likenesses and applies them to life's situations, with stunning results.

In reading this book, you will accelerate out of the pit as you discover how quickly you can transform a stalled, humdrum life into an exciting race. You will then learn to take the curves in the race like an expert as you come to understand how the laws of nature and the laws of the race track can be blended together with Christ-like aggressive behavior, enabling you to pull ahead of those forces that would destroy you if you were not aware of how to win in this race. Finally, Lemons helps you understand how you can glory in the lights and applause of the victory lane and yet still remain humble before God and among those people with whom you live and work.

If you don't have a desire for adventure, for stepping beyond the ordinary, and for experiencing the incredible power of the Spirit of the Living God working in your life, then you should probably cease reading here. If, on the other hand, you are an adventurer in your heart and in your dreams, why not risk reading this book? You'll step out of the bleachers and into the race itself. Rick Lemons has been there. He has seen and experienced the race firsthand. Don't miss the challenge that you will find by reading *The Race—From Pit Row to Victory Lane.*

—**Paige Patterson**
President
Southwestern Baptist Theological Seminary
Fort Worth, Texas

Prologue

One of the fastest growing sports in America is the NASCAR Cup Series. Sometimes as many as 200,000 people sit in the hot sun all day, watching forty-three cars go around in a circle. For those people, and for the hundreds of thousands more who watch on television, seeing the drivers riding each other's bumpers at such high speeds, close enough to read the fine print on their fellow competitors' driving suits, is very entertaining. Yet what happens on the track is a team effort among the ownership, driver, and pit crew. They work together in each race, with the shared goal of ending up in Victory Lane.

In like manner, the Christian life is compared to a race. "Therefore, since we are surrounded by such a great cloud of witnesses, let us throw off everything that hinders and the sin that so easily entangles, and let us run with perseverance the race marked out for us. Let us fix our eyes on Jesus, the author and perfecter of our faith, who for the joy set before him endured the cross, scorning its shame, and sat down at the right hand of the throne of God" (Hebrews 12:1–2). In these verses, the writer of Hebrews exhorts believers to run with patience and keep their eyes on the finish line.

"Do you not know that in a race all the runners run, but only one gets the prize? Run in such a way as to get the prize. Everyone who competes in the games goes into strict training. They do it to get a crown that will not last, but we do it to get a crown that will last forever. Therefore, I do not run like a man running aimlessly; I do not fight like a man beating the air. No, I beat my body and make it my slave so that after I have preached to others, I myself will not be disqualified for the prize" (1 Corinthians 9:24–27).

The apostle Paul writes that we should run to win and practice self-discipline in order to achieve the prize. Both the illustration in Hebrews and the one in 1 Corinthians apply to a foot race where contestants compete individually against other runners. In a NASCAR race, drivers and pit crews compete against other *teams*—and only one team wins the prize.

The Bible uses other metaphors to describe the Christian life. Through the centuries, Bible teachers have used illustrations from their cultures as well. Jesus used illustrations from the first century culture. He spoke of sheep and shepherds, coins and sons. He often spoke in parables to illustrate the kingdom of God and the end of time. He once used the analogy of a person sowing seeds on four types of soil to illustrate the different ways people hear and respond to God's Word.

Many things that happen in a NASCAR race also parallel things that happen in our Christian life. We are involved in our own races, and like those who compete on Sunday at Talladega, Daytona, and Texas Motor Speedway, we need the entire team to succeed. Our race is a partnership among the owner (God), the driver (you), and the pit crew (other believers). God wants you to run the race well. We will explore some of the ways God will help you to do that in this book. Are you in the race? What kind of race are you running?

This book is divided into two sections: Pit Stops and Pitfalls. Every NASCAR team has a pit crew that services the car during the race. Members of that crew concentrate on improving the car throughout the entire race in order to finish well. They keep the car properly fueled, make track-bar adjustments, and change four tires in less than twenty seconds. God also provides our needs for the race of life. Part one of the book will address how the Word of God (the Bible), worship, and prayer are like fuel, tires, and getting instructions from your crew chief.

Part two will address pitfalls. Many things that happen in a race can keep a car from reaching Victory Lane. In life, obstacles and pitfalls also keep us from victory. God wants you to experience a life of victory, here and now. Unfortunately, many believers do not live in victory; they may *believe* in victory, but they do not *enjoy* it. Their lives are wrecked, and some of them are disqualified right out of the gate, before they have an opportunity to succeed. Part two will address some common pitfalls and how you can avoid them.

What exactly is meant by "live in victory"? To live in victory is to live the life that God promised for us. "For everyone born of God overcomes the world. This is the victory that has overcome the world, even our faith. Who is it that overcomes the world? Only he who believes that Jesus is the Son of God" (I John 5:4–5).

To overcome the world implies living by godly principles as opposed to living by the world's view. The world's view and God's view are opposite. The world's view says that man is the measure of all things, and that the way to achieve greatness in life is to assert yourself. God's view is summed up in the words of Jesus Christ: "But many who are first will be last, and many who are last will be first" (Matthew 19:30).

Jesus taught that the way to be great in heaven is to be a servant on earth. This view is contrary to the world's view. The victorious Christian life refuses to bow to the world's view. We must strive to live by the high standards of God's Word. We should not settle for just getting to Victory Lane, if along the way we do not enjoy the ride as well. The Christian race should be enjoyed. Jesus came to bring abundant life. The abundant life He promised is for today as well as eternity. Between the beginning of the race and arriving in Victory Lane, there are many pit stops to make.

If you are ready to begin the race then, "Gentlemen, start your engines!"

Introduction
Gentlemen, Start Your Engines!

Therefore, since we are surrounded by such a great cloud of witnesses, let us throw off everything that hinders and the sin that so easily entangles, and let us run with perseverance the race marked out for us. Let us fix our eyes on Jesus, the author and perfecter of our faith, who for the joy set before him endured the cross, scorning its shame, and sat down at the right hand of the throne of God" (Hebrews 12:1–2).

Perhaps the most excitement that occurs in a NASCAR race happens early on and normally follows the National Anthem. Everyone is excited when the starter declares, "Gentlemen, start your engines!" Whether it's the voice of a NASCAR official, a television celebrity, or a politician coming through the loudspeaker, the crowd is abuzz. Adrenalin pumps through everyone watching and participating in the race. The sound of forty-three cars revving their engines over the roar of fans makes grown men act like little children.

Starting the engine is necessary to participate in the race. A racecar cannot participate without the engine running, no matter how well painted or groomed. Countless hours are spent making the car shine and look attractive for its sponsors and fans, but without sufficient horsepower, the car will not run around the track.

The Holy Spirit is the equivalent of the engine in the life of a believer. In this chapter, I want to help you activate the Holy Spirit in your life, because trying to live the Christian life without the Holy Spirit is like trying to drive an automobile without an engine. Can you imagine someone buying a car without an engine? Imagine for a moment that someone purchased a car for the looks and stereo equipment without any knowledge about how to operate an automobile. Imagine the person pushing their car to work or to your house to show off the sound system. It would be exhausting and pointless to own a car that had to be pushed everywhere. But suppose someone explains that, by placing the key into the ignition and turning on the engine, the car's power can be activated. The owner can go faster, climb hills, and go places he or she has never been before.

That analogy may sound foolish, but that is exactly how many believers run the race of life. They never activate the power of the Holy Spirit. Believers who have discovered God's power through the companion of the Holy Spirit are passing those who are pushing solely with their own strength. Activating the Holy Spirit in your life will enable you to do things you cannot do alone. Life without God is hopeless for an unbeliever, but so is life without engaging the power of the Holy Spirit in the life of a believer. The Holy Spirit lives within each believer: "And if anyone does not have the Spirit of Christ, he does not belong to Christ" (Romans 8:9).

Having an engine under the hood and actually starting it are two different things, and so are possessing the Holy Spirit and activating the Holy Spirit. In Hebrews, chapter 12, the Bible provides instruction on how to run the race and how to activate the Holy Spirit in your life. Activating the Holy Spirit in your life calls for preparation, perseverance, and patterning your life after the life of Jesus Christ.

PREPARATION

"Throw off everything that hinders and the sin that so easily entangles" (Hebrews 12:1). Runners understand the importance of discarding all clothing that will interfere in a race. Many times track and field events take place in spring when the weather is cool outside. Athletes wear warm clothing before their event, but when the time comes for the race, they take off the warm clothes and run in tight clothing. They discard anything that will interfere with their stride. This is the imagery in Hebrews, chapter 12.

Racecar mechanics also spend time preparing the engine for a race. Just as a mechanic will tune an engine in order to maximize the horsepower, the believer also requires daily tune-ups to allow the Holy Spirit to empower his or her life. There are three verses in the New Testament that speak directly to empowering the Holy Spirit in your life.

"So I say, live by the spirit, and you will not gratify the desires of the sinful nature. For the sinful nature desires what is contrary to the Spirit, and the Spirit what is contrary to the sinful nature" (Galatians 5:16–17).

When, by faith, a person accepts Christ's death on the cross as payment for his or her sins, he or she immediately receives the Holy Spirit (Romans 8:9). But according to Paul in Galatians 5:16–17, the person still has the old sinful nature as well. These two natures are opposite and continually war against one another. Jesus said to Peter, "the spirit is willing, but the body (flesh) is weak" (Matthew 26:41).

Paul acknowledged his own struggle with the nature of sin. Romans 7:18: "For I have the desire to do what is good, but I cannot carry it out." He explains in the same chapter that this was not him, but it was sin living in him that caused him not to do the good he wanted to do and often to do the very evil that he no longer wanted to do (verse 20). Most believers can relate to this struggle. We often blame Satan for things that are the result of our own sinful nature. Satan is an enemy to the Christian, but so is our sin nature.

"But each one is tempted when, by his own evil desire, he is dragged away and enticed" (James 1:14).

To combat our sin nature, Paul says we are to "live by the spirit." He is exhorting us to allow the Spirit to control rather than allowing the sin nature to control. *You have a choice.* Before you met Christ, you only had the sin nature, but since you have received Christ, you now have the Spirit (Divine Nature) to assist you. One little boy explained, "When sin knocks at the door, I have two men I can send to the door. I can send the old man or the new man. If I send the old man, then I will sin, but if I send the new man, I will not sin."

This is how you must defeat the sin nature—through submitting to the Spirit and by allowing the Spirit to control your life. We are taught to be more committed, but victory is more about being *sub*mitted than being *com*mitted. The Spirit is able to easily defeat the sin nature, but He will not force His control over your life. We make the choice to allow the Holy Spirit to defeat our sin nature by submitting ourselves to His control. The first thing you can do to prepare for the race is to "submit to the Spirit."

"And do not grieve the Holy Spirit of God, with whom you were sealed for the day of redemption" (Ephesians 4:30).

The second step in activating the Holy Spirit in your life involves a negative command. Paul writes, "Do not grieve the Holy Spirit." The Holy Spirit is the third person of the Godhead and is a living personality. Some consider the Holy Spirit to be an object. Yet Jesus said in John 16:13, "But when he, the Spirit of truth, comes, he will guide you into all truth. He will not speak on his own, he will speak only what he hears, and he will tell you what is yet to come." Five times Jesus used the pronoun "He" to make it clear that the Holy Spirit is a person and not an object. As a person, the Spirit can be grieved. We know that when God is grieved, He withholds His blessings along with His power. Many times in the Old Testament, God warned the nation of Israel that their sin was withholding His blessings. "But your iniquities have separated you from your God; your sins have hidden His face from you so that He will not hear" (Isaiah 59:2).

Sin grieves God. Sin limits the Holy Spirit's work in our lives, much like an engine failing to hit on all cylinders. The Holy Spirit does not leave us when we sin, but He is not as free to work through us as when we are submissive to Him.

We also activate God's power through confession of our sin: "If we confess our sins, he is faithful and just and will forgive our sins and purify us from all unrighteousness" (I John 1:9).

To confess means to agree. God requires us to agree with Him regarding our sin, in order to forgive our sin and reactivate the Holy Spirit's power in our lives. When we refuse to acknowledge our sin or confess our sin, we are in disagreement with God. If we admit our sin and say the same thing God says about our sin, we are immediately forgiven, and the power of the Spirit works in our lives once again.

Are you being honest with God about your sin? You can't hide your sin from God. He lives in us. He is aware of everything happening in our lives. You may be able to hide your sin from others or even yourself, but you cannot hide sin from God. The best thing we can do is to agree with God about our sin and stop trying to defend our sinful conduct.

Sometimes people want to excuse their sin because they see others doing the same thing. They may think their actions do not affect anyone. Whatever the case, as long as you refuse to acknowledge your sin, you will not experience the power of the Spirit-filled life. Thus, the second step to activating the Holy Spirit in your life is to confess your sin so that the Holy Spirit is not grieved.

"Do not put out the Spirit's fire" (1 Thessalonians 5:19).

The third step in activating the Holy Spirit in your life also involves a negative command. "Do not put out the spirit's fire." One translation says: "Do not quench the Holy Spirit" (KJV). The Holy Spirit works *in* your life so that He can work *through* your life. He wants to glorify Christ to the world, and the best we can hope for as believers is to not get in His way. We get in the Holy Spirit's way when we do not confess our sins. Furthermore, we put out the Spirit's fire in our lives when we fail to obey the Spirit's promptings. Each day our companion, the Holy Spirit, leads us and guides us in life. Jesus said in John, chapter 16, that the Spirit prompts us from Scripture. He sometimes uses the small voice living within us, especially when He prompts us to share a word with someone about Christ or to help support a missionary in a foreign country. In everything, we should be sensitive to the Spirit's promptings so that we can live in obedience to God. The more we obey God, the more we can expect God to lead us—and God blesses obedience.

If a fuel line is clogged or broken between the fuel tank and the engine, the engine will not run. Many times the power of the Holy Spirit does not work through us because we are being disobedient to things He asks us to do. We have clogged the line by refusing to be obedient. The old hymn says: "Trust and obey, for there's no other way to be happy in Jesus but to trust and obey." The third step in activating the Holy Spirit in your life is to "obey the spirit's promptings." Are you living in obedience to God? Do you respond with "Yes Lord" when God speaks? Has God given you an assignment that you have refused to obey? Before you can activate the Holy Spirit in your life, you must learn to obey His promptings.

The apostle Paul had Holy Spirit power in his life. He was faithful to obey the spirit's promptings.

Paul and his companions traveled throughout the region of Phrygia and Galatia, having been kept by the Holy Spirit from preaching the word in the province of Asia. When they came to the border of Mysia, they tried to enter Bithynia, but the Spirit of Jesus would not allow them to. So they passed by Mysia and went down to Troas. During the night Paul had a vision of a man of Macedonia standing and begging him, "Come over to Macedonia and help us." After Paul had seen the vision, we got ready at once to leave for Macedonia, concluding that God had called us to preach the gospel to them.

—Acts 16:6–10

Paul heard the Macedonian call and obeyed the Holy Spirit. Because he was faithful to follow the spirit's prompting, the gospel message spread throughout all of Macedonia.

When I was in college, I went on a mission's trip to the West Indies with a group of students. One afternoon we divided into groups of two to go into different neighborhoods to share the gospel. Jerry Johnson, the current president of Criswell College, and I went into the area we had been assigned. We came to a cross-section in the road and had to make a decision quickly about which direction we would take. We prayed about which way to go and decided to turn right rather than left. We both felt the Holy Spirit was leading us to go that way. In the first home we approached lived a man named Baptist Conover. When we told him who we were and why we were there, he told us that we had been sent by God. Just minutes before he had been sitting in his living room with a loaded revolver, thinking about taking his own life. He had prayed to God to send someone to help him, and we showed up. When you obey the Holy Spirit's promptings you can witness amazing things.

PERSEVERANCE

The writer of the book of Hebrews exhorts us: "Let us run with perseverance the race marked out for us" (Hebrews 12:1). Great patience is required to drive in a NASCAR event. I get angry and impatient just driving in normal traffic. Normal people can turn into monsters when they get into an automobile. They will cut you off in traffic, avoid traffic signs, and pretend they didn't see you. Racecar drivers *have* to be very patient. Sometimes the race lasts five hundred miles, at temperatures that exceed 100 degrees. More than patience is required. Perseverance is needed to finish. When the driver gets into the car, he understands it is going to be a long day. Anything can happen, and the driver that perseveres well has the best chance to finish well.

In the Christian race, God has marked out for each person his or her own race. Ours is not a competitive race. We are not in competition with other believers to finish first, but we are compelled to finish *well*. Every person has been designed by God and placed in the race marked out for him or her. Racecar drivers understand that some days they simply do not have the best car on the track. You need to understand that God does not judge you by what others do. There are people in the race who have more gifts and talents than we do, and God does not expect us to compete with them. God expects us to do the best we can with what we have received, and He judges us by how we use what we've received to respond to Him.

In the parable of the talents, Jesus taught in Matthew 25:14–30 that three different men were given different numbers of talents. One man received five talents, another received two talents, and one man was entrusted with only one talent. The master did not expect the man who had received two talents to do as much as the man who'd received five. Nor did the master expect the man who had received one to do as much as the man who had received two, but he *did* expect each one to do something with what he had received. Don't get discouraged if, along the way, you see someone else ahead of you in the race, because he or she may have different equipment that enables him or her to be in that position. Just do the best you can with what God has entrusted to you. Run the race that is set before you, and try not to concern yourself with what everyone around you does.

In John, chapter 21, Jesus had a conversation with Peter about Peter's future. Jesus told Peter that one day he would be led to a place where he did not want to go. Jesus was referring to the way Peter would die. Peter was okay with that. He accepted the race that God marked out for him, but then he asked Jesus about his friend, John. "What about John?" Peter asked. Here is what Jesus said to Peter: "If I want him to remain alive until I return, what is that to you? You must follow me" (John 21:22).

Far too often we are like Peter, and we are more concerned about what God is doing, or wants to do, in someone else's life than we are with those same questions in our own lives. The race that God has designed for you is "marked out." This means that He decides your race to run. In NASCAR, there are different tracks—short tracks, super speedways, and road courses. You should leave up to God which course He sets before you. You will have a lot more peace than when you are concerning yourself with what is happening in someone else's life. Accept the race that God has marked out for *you*, and do your best with what you're given.

PATTERN

"Let us fix our eyes on Jesus" (Hebrews 12:2).

No one ran a better race than Jesus. There is no greater example of how to run the race than Jesus Christ. He was given a race from the Heavenly Father, and He accepted His race with joy. We must keep our eyes on Him all the way through the finish line.

Jesus was the most focused person to ever run the race. He knew exactly what He was sent to do, and He was not sidetracked by the pitfalls along the way. The cross was His mission in life, and He refused to be distracted, even when Peter tried to convince him not to go to Jerusalem. Jesus spoke the harshest words He ever spoke to the twelve when he said to Peter, "Get behind me, Satan!" (Mark 8:33). Jesus recognized that Peter's words were from Satan. Satan had tried earlier to distract Jesus from going to the cross when he tempted Him in the desert. He offered Jesus the world if He would bow to him. Jesus recognized that Satan was trying to distract Him in the desert, and again through the words of Peter.

Like Jesus, we have been sent here from the Heavenly Father to complete our life's mission. We have a divine calling to do what God has sent us to do. Your life has a purpose. Have you discovered your purpose in life? Are you living according to your purpose? Has Satan distracted you from what you are here to do? Being distracted is so easy, and in the second half of this book I will address some of the pitfalls Satan uses to distract us.

Not only was Jesus focused, but also He was faithful. "He endured the cross" (Hebrews 12:2).

Jesus finished His work, and then He sat down at the right hand of God. He did not fall short of doing what He was sent to do. Jesus could have easily given in to the crowd and come down from the cross to avoid the shame of the crucifixion. But He finished. He was faithful. He said while hanging on the cross, "It is finished." Just as Jesus finished His race, we too can finish ours. We must finish! The question then becomes, very simply, *how* will you finish?

Conclusion

Prepare yourself today for the race by activating the power of the Holy Spirit in your life. The best way to prepare is to submit to God and agree with God about your sin. Don't make excuses for your sin. And when the Spirit prompts you to do something, make the choice to obey. Be patient, and understand that the race will be life-long. There will be many things to discourage and defeat you along the way. Can you accept that you are not in competition with others and run the race that God has marked out for you? You *can* finish, no matter what others do.

Pattern yourself after Jesus, who remained focused and faithful in the race the Heavenly Father marked out for Him. Learn all about the way Jesus lived His life. Spend time with Him in prayer, and study His Word so you can know Him better.

The race is before you today. Are you prepared? Have you started your engine?

PART I
PIT STOPS

Are You Running on Empty?

The date was May 2, 2004, and the place was the California Speedway. Bobby Labonte pitted on lap 199 of the 250-lap Auto Club 500. By lap 222, the number 18 car moved into second place behind leader Jeff Gordon. By lap 248, he had trimmed Gordon's lead to less than two seconds and was within striking distance of his first Cup victory of the season. However, as Labonte chased Gordon into turn 1, his car ran out of fuel, and he coasted more than a mile to the start/finish line. Labonte finished a disappointing fifth.

The most important ingredient to a racecar's engine is fuel. A car cannot run without an engine, and an engine cannot operate without fuel. Every gas-powered engine requires fuel. Once, on a typical August day in Texas, I was mowing my lawn. The temperature was about 102 degrees outside, with a temperature humidity index of 110. I was halfway finished with the yard, completely covered with perspiration, when the tractor stopped running. I tried everything I knew to restart the engine, but nothing worked. After repeated attempts to start the engine, the battery died. I decided to check the fuel tank. Sure enough, the tank was empty. After a trip to the gas station and a boost for the battery, I was back in business. The inconvenience of running out of fuel, however, had made me late for an evening appointment.

There is a lot of strategy in determining how much fuel and the type of fuel required to operate a racecar in certain climates. If the crew calculates correctly, there will be just enough to finish the race and perhaps to allow the driver to cut a few donuts on the sponsor's emblem in the infield before taking one last victory lap around the track. But if they miscalculate the amount of fuel, they can end up like Bobby Labonte at the 2004 Auto Club 500. Running out of fuel can be very embarrassing, along with costing points toward the Cup at the end of the year.

You and I require fuel to run the Christian race. Our fuel is the Word of God. If you plan to succeed in life, then you must make frequent fuel stops in God's Word. Unlike NASCAR Teams that take as few fuel stops as necessary, you must make frequent fuel stops. NASCAR teams fuel quickly, but you should spend as much time as possible in the Word of God in order to run a good race.

God's Word is compared to spiritual milk. "Like newborn babies, crave pure spiritual milk, so that by it you may grow up in your salvation" (1 Peter 2:2). Peter understood the importance of God's Word. He encourages us to crave the Word of God much the same as an infant craves milk. Ann and I have a new granddaughter, Isabella Faith Davis. She is our first of what we hope will be many. Isabella loves her milk. When she is hungry, a warm bottle of milk is the only thing that will satisfy her. When she is taking her bottle of milk, she is satisfied. When she craves milk, nothing else will satisfy her. Not water! Not juice! Only milk! In the same way, believers should crave the Word of God.

The Word of God is food for our souls. God's Word will sustain you in the race. Some try to operate on emotionalism. They believe they can go to church on Sunday and get fueled for the week. They depend on a worship leader or a pastor to excite them enough to remain energized through the upcoming week. They think attending church is like making a spiritual pit stop. Emotions are good, but emotions change. People who operate on emotions often run out of fuel before the end of the race. Many in the crowd who cried, "Crucify Jesus," on Friday had cried, "Hosanna," to Him just five days earlier. Their emotions changed with the tide of popular opinion. Emotions are part of who we are, but emotions cannot be the fuel that operates your Christian life.

Others depend on people to help them finish the race. They expect relationships and accountability groups to keep them in the race. Healthy relationships and accountability are important, but they will not keep you in the race. Your soul requires frequent nourishment from the Word of God. When the nation of Israel came out of captivity in Babylon, the people returned to Jerusalem to rebuild the Temple and the wall that surrounded the city for protection. This is the way Nehemiah explained it:

When the seventh month came and the Israelites had settled in their towns, all the people gathered as one man in the square before the Water Gate. They told Ezra the scribe to bring out the Book of the Law of Moses, which the Lord had commanded for Israel. So on the first day of the seventh month Ezra the priest brought the Law before the assembly, which was made up of men and women and all who were able to understand. He read it aloud from daybreak till noon as he faced the square before the Water Gate in the presence of the men, women and others who could understand. And all the people listened attentively to the Book of the Law.

—Nehemiah 8:1–3

That is impressive! Many pastors would welcome the opportunity to preach a sermon from daybreak till noon and not hear people complain. Instead of complaining, the people of Israel listened attentively. They had been without the public reading of the Law for many years. The drought had left them hungry to hear God's Word. When Ezra read the Law, this was like placing a bottle in the mouth of an infant who had missed his or her last feeding. The law of God was what they craved. Every born again believer should crave the Word of God.

There comes a time when a believer must grow beyond the elementary things (milk) and move on to what the Bible calls "solid food."

"Brothers, I could not address you as spiritual but as worldly—mere infants in Christ. I gave you milk, not solid food, for you were not ready for it" (1 Corinthians 3:1–2).

The believers in the city of Corinth were having issues. The church in Corinth was one of the most immature churches of the first century. Most of their problems, such as abusing the Lord's Supper, dragging fellow believers to court, and the abuse of the gift of tongues can be traced to what Paul wrote in the above verses. They were still infants in Christ when they should have grown past milk to solid food. While children are growing, a parent must be careful not to give food they are unprepared to digest. But as children grow, they require solid food. The Bible contains milk for the young, solid food for the spiritually mature, and everything in between. Adrian Rogers, longtime pastor of The Bellevue Baptist Church in Cordova, Tennessee, once said, "The

Bible is like an ocean. It is shallow enough that a little child can wade in it and yet deep enough for theologians to drown."

There is something for every level of spiritual maturity in the Bible. The goal for all believers should be to grow in knowledge. We must not be content with milk; we must crave God's Word like an infant craves milk. Sometimes I crave a big juicy steak. What about you?

In order to crave God's Word, we must understand the importance of God's Word and the intent of God's Word.

The Importance of God's Word

The Bible does not merely contain God's Word; it *is* God's Word, His Word to and for us. When you read the Bible, you are reading the Word God has for your life. He speaks to us through the pages of Scripture, and He energizes our lives through the encouraging stories of faith we read in the Bible. "These things happened to them as examples and were written down as warnings for us, on whom the fulfillment of the ages has come" (1 Corinthians 10:11). The apostle Paul reminds us that every story God included in the Bible is written for us. There are lessons to be learned from the stories of the past. God has specifically included each story for our benefit.

There are two very important passages in the New Testament that speak directly to the importance of God's Word.

First, "All Scripture is God-breathed and is useful for teaching, rebuking, correcting and training in righteousness, so that the man of God may be thoroughly equipped for every good work" (2 Timothy 3:16–17).

The Bible is more than a book of lessons or inspirational stories. Every word comes to us through divine inspiration, without error. God's Word is reliable and relevant for our lives today. Even though the Bible was written over centuries and centuries ago, it is still relevant and will remain relevant until Christ returns. God never changes, and His Word remains the same. One motivation for making frequent fuel stops in the Word of God is that, when you read the Bible, you are hearing from God.

Second, "Above all, you must understand that no prophecy of Scripture came about by the prophet's own interpretation. For prophecy never had its origin in the will of man, but men spoke from God as they were carried along by the Holy Spirit" (2 Peter 1:20–21).

Peter explains to us how the Bible came to be God-breathed. He wrote that God the Holy Spirit carried each writer along so that what he wrote was exactly what God intended. There is uniqueness about each book of the Bible that involves the personality of the author, but God did not leave the writing up to the author. Through divine inspiration, God used the individual personality of the writer, but His Holy Spirit inspired every word. This can be seen in the different accounts of the life of Christ as told in the four gospels—Matthew, Mark, Luke, and John. Each writer tells the same story but to a different audience and with different style. Yet their stories are harmonious and accurate. Zig Ziglar once said, "If four men saw the same accident on a street corner, in less than five minutes you would have four different accounts of what happened." In the Bible, four different men wrote about events that transpired over three and one-half years almost thirty years after the fact. Their stories harmonize because they had one source of information—the Holy Spirit. Jesus said, "All this I have spoken to you while still with you. But the Counselor, the Holy Spirit, whom the Father will send in my name, will teach you all things and will remind you of everything I have said while still with you" (John 14:25–26).

The Holy Spirit was the one who reminded the writers of the gospels about everything that Jesus said and did. So while there were four different writers, there was only one author—the Holy Spirit. What was true of the four gospels is also true of the entire Bible. Each time we read the Bible we can be sure we are reading God's divine Word, and it is exactly what we need for today.

But there is more.

"Your word is a lamp to my feet and a light for my path" (Psalm 119:105). God wants to guide your life through the Bible. The Word of God is like a lamp that lights the way ahead of us so we can walk clearly. God speaks to us today through counsel we receive and through the experiences of life, but these things are not always reliable. We can receive mixed signals when we rely only on counsel or when we are trying to discern God's will from the experiences of life. God's Word is reliable. God's Word has been tried and proven over the ages. Everything a person hears must be examined against Scripture. The Bible is compared to a light that shines the way. Reading the Bible is like driving an automobile at night. The headlights on the car illuminate a portion of the road where you are going. You can't see everything ahead of you, but you can see enough to continue. The longer you continue, the more of the road you see. Each day God is giving us direction and guidance for our lives, and as much as we need God's Word to nourish our souls, we also need God's Word to help us see the way He wants us to go.

There are two methods for receiving God's direction from the Bible. The first is through Bible reading. The Bible should be read as it was written, in books. Many people make New Year's resolutions to read through the Bible in one year. This is a good way to read the Bible. There are resources available today to assist you in reading through the Bible. When you sit down to read the Bible, you have the opportunity to meet with God. Make it a practice at times to just read and let the Lord speak to you. Don't read with the intention of preparing a lesson or to gain more knowledge. Simply read the Bible and pay attention to what God is saying to you. You can begin with this simple prayer: "Lord speak to me today as I read from your Word." This is called a "quiet time." Every believer needs some alone time with God in order to hear God's Word for his or her life.

The second method for receiving God's direction is through Bible study. This is where you are digging a little deeper and seeking more understanding of a verse or passage. The difference between Bible reading and Bible study is compared to the difference between flying over a city and driving through a city in the Navigators "Growing Strong in God's Family." On page forty of the 2:7 series, they explain:

> Bible reading is like flying over a city and looking at streets and buildings but not really paying attention to the names and addresses. Bible study is like taking the time to drive thru the neighborhoods. You look at the architecture of the buildings and you identify the addresses on the buildings along with the names of the streets. Bible study requires

that you dig deeper into the words and context of the Scripture in order to understand it better. Believers should study the Bible in order to know God better and to grow in knowledge.

You should consider doing both Bible reading and Bible study, because both are important to the Christian life. You should not neglect either method. You can get so involved in a Bible study that you do not take the time to listen to God. However if you are only interested in reading the Bible without *studying* the Bible, you are doing a disservice to your walk with God. You are neglecting the importance of learning more about the Bible and may not grow in the knowledge of God. Both Bible reading and Bible study are healthy for the Christian life. Each provides the spiritual fuel we need to run the race. Reserve time in your life for both.

The Intent of God's Word

In 1 Peter 2:2, the apostle Peter instructed believers to crave God's Word "so that you may grow." A believer not growing in Christ is unfortunate. We begin the Christian life as infants, but God expects us to grow beyond infancy to maturity. When I was younger, I attended Vacation Bible School each summer. All the children would line up in the parking lot in their different age groups to go marching into the Worship Center on cue. This was a tradition in our church. Each group would sit together by age and file in to the song, "Onward Christian Soldiers." As the years passed, we would move from group to group. All the first graders lined up in a row and the second graders beside them. For the most part, all the children were about the same size, until you looked over at the fifth grade class. In line with the fifth graders was a man about age thirty. His name was Bobby, and everyone knew him. He did not attend our church on Sundays, but he was at every Vacation Bible School I can recall. And he was always in the fifth grade class. Even though Bobby grew physically, he never grew mentally beyond the fifth grade. Most of the time, the other fifth graders were kind to him. We grew past the fifth grade, but he never did.

That story is close to home for many. Perhaps you can relate. Maybe you know someone like Bobby. He was mentally challenged and had no choice. This was not his fault. He did the best he could. There are believers like him. They have been believers for years, but they are not maturing in their faith. They are stuck on a certain level. Unlike Bobby, we have the ability to grow spiritually, but some refuse. They choose not to grow. Why would a person choose not to grow in Christ? That person may not know he or she can grow. There are some believers who think you have to attend seminary or have a degree in the Bible in order to study God's Word. God has written His Word so that we can understand it. He has provided all the assistance we need by giving us His Holy Spirit to be our guide and teacher. The Holy Spirit stands ready to help you understand the Bible. He is committed to your spiritual growth.

God has given His Word to help us grow. God's Word is a rock-solid foundation upon which you can build your life. Jesus once mentioned two types of builders (Matthew 7:24–27). One man was foolish because he built his house on the sand. When the winds blew and the storms came, the man's house was destroyed, because it was not built on a solid foundation. However, the other man was wise because he built his house on a rock. Because the foundation was strong, when the winds blew and the storms came, the man's house remained. The most solid foundation for your Christian life is the Word of God. "All men are like grass, and all their glory is like the flowers of the field; the grass withers and the flowers fall, but the word of the Lord stands forever" (1 Peter 1:24–25).

God's Word is a strong enduring foundation. God's Word has withstood every attack and will remain secure. Be like the wise man and build your life on the solid foundation of God's Word. God's Word will outlast your time on this earth and will make the time you spend on this earth more secure. Learn to be a good listener when God speaks to you from the Bible.

> A farmer went out to sow his seed. As he was scattering the seed, some fell along the path, and the birds came and ate it up. Some fell on rocky places, where it did not have much

soil. It sprang up quickly, because the soil was shallow. But when the sun came up, the plants were scorched, and they withered because they had no root. Other seed fell among thorns, which grew up and choked the plants. Still other seed fell on good soil, where it produced a crop—a hundred, sixty or thirty times what was sown.

—Matthew 13:3–8

Listen then to what the parable of the sower means: When anyone hears the message about the kingdom and does not understand it, the evil one comes and snatches away what was sown in his heart. This is the seed sown along the path. The one who received the seed that fell on rocky places is the man who hears the word and at once receives it with joy. But since he has no root, he lasts only a short time. When trouble or persecution comes because of the word, he quickly falls away. The one who received the seed that fell among thorns is the man who hears the word, but the worries of this life and the deceitfulness of wealth choke it, making it unfruitful. But the one who received the seed that fell on good soil is the man who hears the word and understands it. He produces a crop, yielding a hundred, sixty or thirty times what was sown.

—Matthew 13:18–23

In this story Jesus spoke of four types of listeners:

First there is the person who has been hardened. This person's heart is hardened by sin and situations that occurred in life. The Word of God never penetrates his or her heart. Before the Word penetrates this person's heart, Satan steals the Word away. This person's heart is so hardened by the trials and tribulations of life that he or she does not hear God. God is speaking, but the enemy snatches away the truth before the truth has the opportunity to change the person's life.

The second listener is the one who hears with joy but does not last. There are people who seem to understand God's Word. They hear the Word of God, and they embrace the truth with a lot of emotion. Because they are only emotional listeners, they do not last. I have been a pastor for thirty years. I have personally witnessed many emotional listeners. There are people who respond very emotionally to what they hear. They leave church with reckless abandonment, but as they run out of emotions, or when their emotions change, they soon fall out of the race. They start well, but they do not finish well.

The third listener is the one who has the seed choked out by clutter in his or her life. This person has filled his or her life with things that do not satisfy. These things keep this person from hearing God. He is speaking, but this person does not hear because he or she is pre-occupied by other things. There is nothing wrong with having the things money can buy so long as you have the thing that money cannot buy. Possessions can get in the way of our hearing from God. But so can other things. Many times, good things can get in the way of our hearing from Him. One time Jesus visited the town of Bethany, where Mary and Martha, the sisters of Lazarus, lived. Martha was a servant at heart. She took great pride in preparing things for Jesus. She cooked, and she cleaned the house to make sure everything was just right for Jesus. Mary, on the other hand, sat at Jesus' feet. This probably implies that Jesus was teaching and Mary was listening rather than helping Martha in the kitchen. Martha spoke to Jesus about Mary. She asked Jesus to tell Mary to help her. Here is what Jesus said to Martha: "Martha, Martha, you are worried and upset about many things, but only one thing is needed. Mary has chosen what is better, and it will not be taken away from her" (Luke 10:40–41).

I have always heard that when Jesus calls your name twice, it is like using your middle name. When I was a child and I got into trouble, my mother always called me by both my first and middle name. When I heard my middle name, I knew I was in trouble. Martha was worried and upset by many things. The tragedy is that those things kept her from listening to Jesus. Sure, someone had to do the cooking and the cleaning, but there would be time for those things later. The Son of God does not come to your home every day. Is your life cluttered with things that keep you from hearing today?

The fourth listener is the type of listener every believer should aspire to be. This person hears the Word, and because he or she has prepared to hear the Word by cultivating his or her heart to God, the seed produces a healthy crop. When God speaks, this one is prepared to hear.

This person hears and receives God's Word. The Word of God produces fruit. The Word of God will keep you going in the race.

A few years back, I was returning from Costa Rica, along with five other pastors, on a Saturday afternoon flight. We had spent the week assisting some American missionaries with a Bible Conference. I was sitting next to one of the pastors who took down a tape-recorder, notepad, and pen from the overhead luggage compartment. He placed the recorder's earpiece in his ear and began to write down some things on the notepad. About thirty minutes later he turned off the recorder and stored everything back in the luggage compartment. He was taking notes from another pastor's sermon in order to preach that same sermon at his church the next day. He then leaned over to me and said, "I guess you think less of me for doing this?" I told him I was not his judge. I related to him that most pastors have preached someone else's sermon before. I shared with him, however, that if this was his weekly custom then he was hurting himself and the church. That may have been a great sermon preached by another man, but God wants to give each one the word He has for us to present. God speaks to us as individuals, and He uses our individuality to speak through us to others. Nothing is as rewarding as discovering the Word of God for oneself and presenting God's Word to others. God's Word is an age-old message, but the message is fresh to you when you dig the message out for yourself. Not long after, my friend was overtaken by a serious moral failure and left the ministry.

You will need to make frequent fuel stops along the way in order to finish the race well. Not finishing the race is not an option. In the race of life, everyone will finish, but not everyone will finish well. If you will read and study God's Word, you are most likely to finish strong.

Four New Tires 2

At the Homestead-Miami Speedway, a sure victory for Bill Elliott turned into an unbelievable disappointment when a cut tire in the final lap handed the 2003 Ford 400 win to Bobby Labonte. Elliott wound up in eighth and then watched helplessly as the car caught fire after he stopped.

Every racecar team understands the importance of tires to a car's performance. Tires are designed to help cars perform faster, with greater traction. Rarely does a driver pull into pit row without his crew changing the tires. Most of the time they will change all four tires, but on some occasions, in order to make a quicker stop, the crew will change only two. Fresh tires help the car run faster, providing the driver with greater stability during the race. Crews calculate the right amount of air pressure so the car will not be tight or too loose on the track. Good tires are essential for the race.

In the same way that good tires balance an automobile, worship provides the believer with proper balance for the Christian life. Worship can be compared to putting on four new tires. God has invited us to worship Him. Worship allows the believer to experience the joy of the Lord through praise. Many times we go through life deflated like a flat tire. We feel like we are slipping and sliding all over the road. The air has gone out of our lives. Others are passing us by. We want to catch up. We try to hold the car on the track, but we are running on flat tires. If you have ever driven a car that had a blow out, you know how dangerous a blown tire can be. The same happens on the road of life, where you think everything is going well, and all of a sudden the air goes out of your life. During a race, tires can lose pressure, causing the car to lose balance.

Just as racecars make stops for tires, a believer requires times of worship. The trials and hardships of life can cause us to lose balance. Trials can deflate you and make you feel like the air has gone out of your life. Worship is like changing tires. Worship brings balance back into our lives. Man was created to worship God and to bring honor and glory to Him.

"In him we were also chosen, having been predestined according to the plan of him who works out everything in conformity with the purpose of his will, in order that we, who were the first to hope in Christ, might be for the praise of his glory" (Ephesians 1:11–12).

From the very beginning, God's plan was for His creation to offer Him praise. God took pleasure in what He created and wanted His creation to take pleasure in Him. As God looked down upon His creation, He repeatedly said, "It is good" (Genesis 1). There was nothing more pleasing to God than the crown of His creation—the man whom He created. Man is the crown of God's creation because man was created in God's image.

Then God said, "Let us make man in our image, in our likeness, and let them rule over the fish of the sea and the birds of the air, over the livestock, over all the earth, and over all the creatures that move along the ground" (Genesis 1:26).

Man is different from the rest of creation because man is created with a soul that will live forever. Everything God created has His signature, but man bears His image. From the beginning of creation, God has invited man to worship Him. God enjoys our worship. He invites us to live a life defined by worship. Worship can be defined as "worth-ship." As we worship God, we are ascribing to Him the worth rightly belonging to the one who created us and redeemed us by His blood. The idea that a Holy God would desire our worship is most remarkable.

Many think of worship as going to church, where believers meet in corporate worship. This is an important type of worship but should not be the only time we worship God. Public worship should be an overflow of the private worship believers experience daily. We are encouraged in Romans 12:1 to "present our bodies as living sacrifices" because it is "your spiritual act of worship." This indicates worship is part of our lifestyle.

Worship is used both as a noun and a verb in the Bible. A noun is defined as a person, place, or thing. Worship is not a person, even though we worship Jesus Christ. Worship is not a place, because Jesus told the woman at the well in John, chapter 4, where you worship is not what matters but how you worship. Worship is something we do. Worship is what we were created to do.

"Where is the one who has been born king of the Jews? We saw his star in the east and have come to worship Him" (Matthew 2:2).

The wise men had journeyed for a long time and from far away to worship the baby Jesus. This could be their song:

> Here I am to worship
> Here I am to bow down,
> Here I am to say that you're my God.
> You're all together lovely,
> all together worthy,
> All together wonderful to me!

In worship, we present ourselves before Almighty God for His purpose and plan. Our attitude when we worship is one of submission before God. Worship recognizes the sovereignty of God. We bow before Him in total submission to His will. This is the act of worship. Worship is more about surrender than singing. Too much emphasis is being placed on the style of worship rather than the importance of worship. The style of music we sing and the atmosphere of a worship service is more a matter of individual preference. God is not so limited that He only enjoys a certain type of worship style. God invites all believers to "come before Him with joyful songs."

The apostle Paul invites us to "sing psalms, hymns and spiritual songs" (Colossians 3:16). Every believer should participate in the style of praise and worship that allows him or her to express worth to God most effectively. Debating over the issue of worship styles wastes far too much energy. The one requirement for all worship songs is they should be consistent with Scripture. "Let the word of Christ dwell in you richly as you teach and admonish one another with all wisdom, and as you sing psalms, hymns and spiritual songs" (Colossians 3:16). Words put to music and sung to God ought to be doctrinally sound.

Worship is also used as a verb in the Bible. A verb is a word of action. When we worship, we are actively expressing worth to God. Worship requires action.

"Jesus said to him, Away from me, Satan! For it is written: Worship the Lord your God, and serve Him only" (Matthew 4:10).

My intention is not to debate over the style of worship that is most effective. I do, however, hope to point out the importance of worship in your life. Worship should be both private and public. Paul and Silas turned a prison cell into a house of worship: "About midnight Paul and Silas were praying and singing hymns to God, and the other prisoners were listening to them" (Acts 16:25).

You do not have to go to church in order to worship. You can worship God any time and any place. When God does something in your life, you want to worship Him. When God parted the waters of the Red Sea so Israel could cross safely and then released the waters in order to destroy the Egyptians, the nation began to worship: "Then Moses and the Israelites sang this song to the Lord: I will sing to the Lord, for he is highly exalted. The horse and its rider he has hurled into the sea" (Exodus 15:1).

The Israelites had something to sing about. The Lord had destroyed their enemy before their very eyes. They had no other way to escape. They could not go around the Red Sea. There was no time to build a bridge. All they could do was trust God and march forward. As soon as they began to move, God parted the waters. The people marched safely to the other side. The thrill of seeing God work in such a mighty way led the people to worship. When God is active in your life, you cannot help but give Him praise. Many times we allow life's circumstances to interfere with what God created us to do. Worship brings balance. Worship allows you to express to God His "worth-ship" in your life. Worship helps get you back in the race with greater stability. An unbalanced tire can affect the car's performance. An unbalanced life will affect your ability to run the race God has marked out for you.

Worship is not limited to going to church or to the style of music we sing. When we join together with other believers to praise our God, in spite of the difficulties of life, worship helps balance our lives. If you ignore the importance of public worship, then you are like an automobile driving on a flat tire. You can go, but you will not enjoy the ride. Public worship brings us back to the center. Perhaps you have experienced one of life's hardships or trials. Then you are in need of worship. Worship can be like changing four new tires. The Lord invites us to pull into pit row for new tires.

As a pastor, I meet people from all walks of life. Some I would describe as having it all together, while others are in crisis. Many fall somewhere in between. People come to church with a lot of baggage, looking for help. Sometimes they do not even know they need help. The demands of life have caused them to neglect the importance for worship. They may not have intended to neglect worship, but they get so busy doing a lot of good things that they do not have time for the most important things. One such man became a dear friend to me in 1994. I met Kevin Duncan, his wife, Rhonda, and their children for the first time after a Sunday church service. I returned their visit on Monday evening by going to their home. Rhonda was so hospitable, but Kevin did not have any time for me. He was a very busy young man, running a company and managing a business of his own. He was very successful, and at the time, you might say Kevin was not "buying what I was selling."

Rhonda and their children continued to attend our church. I would run into Kevin from time to time in our small community and at other social events. He was always cordial but not interested in attending church. Kevin was a believer. He gave his life to Christ at an early age, but his quest for success did not allow time for worship. Then Kevin discovered he had colon cancer. Suddenly Kevin's priorities shifted. Our lives can change with one phone call or by one visit to the doctor as Kevin's did. He was told he only had about six months to live, but by the grace of God, he lived for over four years. During those four years Kevin became very involved in our church. He was at every church function when he was physically capable. Before he went to be with the Lord, I had the privilege of being among his dearest friends. I watched as the Lord worked in Kevin's life. I saw him struggle, and I saw him try to live for the One who died for him, Jesus Christ. He became a true worshipper. I wouldn't say that Kevin was all that outwardly expressive in his worship. He did not raise his hands or dance in the aisles of our church. He simply discovered that attending weekly times of worship brought balance to his life, and the things that once distracted his attention from worship were set aside for the thing that was the most important.

"Let us not give up meeting together, as some are in the habit of doing, but let us encourage one another—and all the more as you see the Day approaching" (Hebrews 10:25).

You will strengthen your Christian life by being faithful to public worship. Every believer should find a Bible-believing church that understands the importance of worship and get involved. Join with other believers who have discovered the support they receive for the race through worship, fellowship, prayer, and the study of God's Word. These are the basic necessities for the race.

Worship Begins with Praise

Shout for joy to the Lord, all the earth.
Worship the Lord with gladness;
Come before him with joyful songs.
Know that the Lord is God.
It is he who made us, and we are his;
We are his people, the sheep of his pasture.

Enter his gates with thanksgiving
And his courts with praise;
Give thanks to him and praise his name.
For the Lord is good and his love endures forever;
his faithfulness continues through all generations.
—Psalm 100

Webster defines praise as, "To commend the worth of." Worship is defined in Psalm 100:2 as "joyful songs." Every believer can make *joyful* sounds. If God said we were to make a *melodious* song, then some could not worship. There are some people who cannot carry a tune in a bucket. But everyone can make a joyful song. The psalmist explains joyful songs as songs of thanksgiving. Songs that please God come from hearts of thanksgiving. We are exhorted in the Bible to be thankful in everything.

There are times when being thankful is difficult. When the doctor gives you bad news or when tragedy strikes a family member, being thankful is hard. When you have lost a job, or had material possessions destroyed by a fire, being thankful can be difficult. Yet everyone has a reason to give thanks. According to verse five of Psalm 100, "the Lord is good and His love endures forever." The Psalmist emphasizes two things: the Lord is God (verse 3) and the Lord is good (verse 5).

Do you believe that? Many times the hardest thing to admit is that He is God and I am not. When life is difficult and things happen that you don't understand, blaming God is easier than accepting that He is a good God. God is not our religious "bell-hop." He does not exist to jump every time we ring the bell. Man was created according to God's divine plan and not our own. We want to make our life the entire puzzle when, in fact, we are just *part* of the puzzle. The longer I live, the more I realize what a small piece of the puzzle I really am. As long as we are making our life the puzzle rather than a piece of the puzzle, then the more we are likely to go through life being bitter and filled with disappointment. When we learn to thank God for the difficulties in life, then the more of God's peace we will experience.

"Do not be anxious about anything, but in everything by prayer and petition, with thanksgiving, present your requests to God. And the peace of God, which transcends all understanding, will guard your hearts and your minds in Christ Jesus" (Philippians 4:6–7).

If we make our lives all about us rather than all about Him, we are very likely to fall into depression. Depression is often brought on by discouragement, and discouragement often results from unmet expectations.

John the Baptist was the forerunner of Jesus Christ. He was born six months before Jesus. He was sent by God to announce Jesus to the world. He referred to himself as a "friend of the bridegroom" (John 3:29). John's responsibility was to introduce to the world "the Lamb of God that takes away the sins of the world" (John 1:29). John was content with that. He was perfectly fine with decreasing so that Jesus could increase (John 3:30). A day came when John's confidence in Jesus changed. John the Baptist was in prison. He sent two men to ask Jesus this question: "Are you the one who was to come, or should we expect someone else?" (Luke 7:18–19).

The same man who had declared Jesus to be the Messiah was now questioning Him. So what happened? The explanation may be found in Jesus' response: "Go back and report to John what you have seen and heard: The blind receive sight, the lame walk, those who have leprosy are cured, the deaf hear, the dead are raised and the good news is preached to the poor. Blessed is the man who does not fall away on account of me" (Luke 7:22–23).

Perhaps John held the expectation that because he had been faithful to Jesus then Jesus would now be faithful to him. Should He rescue John from prison? Perhaps Jesus knew about John's doubts? Maybe that is why he said to John, "Blessed is the man who does not fall away on account of me." In the end, Jesus knew John would remain faithful because He paid John the Baptist the highest compliment: "I tell you, among those born of women there is no one greater than John" (Luke 7:28).

John's unmet expectation that Jesus would come may have led to his discouragement. His discouragement led him to doubt, and his doubt may have led to depression. I do not believe John would have asked that question if he had been out in the wilderness or standing along the shores of Galilee preaching repentance. While John was locked up behind closed doors, in an environment to which he was not accustomed, was when he began to doubt. John was unlike the apostle Paul, who was as comfortable in prison as he was in the synagogues. Paul preached Christ any place and any time. But John the Baptist was made for the wilderness. John was at his best when he was in the wilderness feeding on locusts and wild honey. He was at his best when he was calling men to repent. He was not comfortable in prison. He was in the wrong environment.

We need to remember when difficult things are happening in our lives, that this does not mean God has abdicated His throne. Jesus told the two messengers to return to John and tell him what was happening. People were being changed by the Son of God whom John had announced to the world. John's own words were being fulfilled: "He must increase and I must decrease." When trials come and you still "sing to the Lord for He is good," you are putting air back in the tires of your life. The road of life may have handed you a flat tire, but you can pull over and get fresh tires by worshipping God, in spite of your circumstances. Praise and worship should not be associated with our circumstances. We give praise because He is God and because He is good.

Praise Leads to God's Presence

Earlier I mentioned the time Paul and Silas were in prison and started to worship. They were in the city of Philippi, when Paul cast a demonic spirit out of a slave girl. This same girl had earned a great deal of money for her owners. They were not very pleased with her new life. They captured Paul and Silas and dragged them into the marketplace to face the authorities. They accused them of throwing the city into an uproar. The authorities ordered Paul and Silas to be stripped and beaten. Once they had been flogged, they were thrown into prison, and their feet were fastened in stocks. This probably implies that Paul and Silas were chained to a cold dungeon floor and lying on their backs in a pool of blood. As they looked up toward the sky at about midnight, they turned that prison cell into a worship center. They began to pray and sing hymns to God. Listen to what happened next: "Suddenly there was such a violent earthquake that the foundations of the prison were shaken. At once all the prison doors flew open, and everybody's chains came loose" (Acts 16:26).

You could say that God showed up! God was pleased with the fact that Paul and Silas could worship in spite of their circumstances. God took hold of that prison and shook it with an earthquake. And no one left. The jailer woke up, and when he saw the prison doors open, he drew his sword and was about to kill himself, because he thought the prisoners had escaped. But Paul shouted, "Don't harm yourself! We are all here!" (Acts 16:27–28).

Do you suppose those people had heard something earlier that they wanted to hear more about? How could two men so severely beaten sing praises? What did they have to sing about? No doubt their singing in spite of their circumstances raised the curiosity of everyone in that prison. When God shows up, there is power. It may seem like midnight in your life. You may be going through a very difficult time right now in your life, but if you will find the strength to praise God in worship, He will come to you. Anyone can worship and sing songs of praise when everything is going well. Faith is needed to sing praises to God when times are difficult.

The story is written in 2 Chronicles 20 about how the armies of Moab and Ammon were threatening the nation of Israel. Some of the men of Israel came and told King Jehoshaphat that a vast army was coming against him from Edom. The people came to seek help from the Lord, and Jehoshaphat stood and prayed:

> O Lord, God of our fathers, are you not the God who is in heaven? You rule over all the kingdoms of the nations. Power and might are in your hand, and no one can withstand you. O our God, did you not drive out the inhabitants of this land before your people Israel and give it forever to the descendents of Abraham your friend? They have lived in it and have built in it a sanctuary for your Name, saying, "If calamity comes upon us, whether the sword of judgment, or plague or famine, we will stand in your presence before this temple that bears your Name and will cry out to you in our distress, and you will hear us and save us."
>
> But now here are men from Ammon, Moab and Mount Seir, whose territory you would not allow Israel to invade when they came from Egypt; so they turned away from them and did not destroy them. See how they are repaying us by coming to drive us out of the possession you gave us as an inheritance? O our God, will you not judge them? For we have no power to face this vast army that is attacking us. We do not know what to do, but our eyes are upon you.
> —2 Chronicles 20:6–12

I feel that way sometimes. I do not know what to do, but my eyes are upon God. You may not know how you are going to make your house payment, but your eyes are still on the Lord. Maybe you do not know how you will get through the treatments the doctor has ordered, but I encourage you to keep your eyes on the Lord. God went on to instruct Israel to put all the male singers in front of the army as they went into this battle. Listen to the words of their song: "Give thanks to the Lord, for His love endures forever" (2 Chronicles 20:21).

They did not know what to do. They believed their circumstance was unchangeable. Yet they gave thanks. As with Paul and Silas, God showed up on that day in Israel's history: "As they began to sing and praise, the Lord set ambushes against the men of Ammon and Moab and Mount Seir who were invading Judah, and they were defeated. The men of Ammon rose up against the men from Mount Seir to destroy and annihilate them. After they finished slaughtering the men from Seir, they helped to destroy one another" (2 Chronicles 20:22–23).

God's presence is what we need in times of trouble. When God is with us, we do not need to be afraid. His presence does not guarantee we will not have trouble, but His presence will give us peace during our trouble. The one who spoke peace to the storm at Galilee can calm the storms in our lives. When you praise Him, He shows up.

On September 30, 1996, our worship leader/student pastor at Fellowship was tragically killed in an automobile accident. Tony Brown was well loved by the people in the congregation. He had been on our church staff for six years and had just celebrated his 28th birthday, along with his first month of marriage. Tony and his beautiful wife, D'Shea, were on their way to Wiggins, Mississippi, after a home Bible study on a Sunday evening. Tony's death raised a lot more questions than I had answers for. How could God allow a young man with so much life ahead of him to die so suddenly? As a pastor, I found myself ministering to the church family, even though I had lost a dear friend and son in the ministry.

It was not until months later that I was able to sit down and reflect on what had happened. I had been so busy trying to console a young wife, students, choir members, and an entire church congregation through the tragedy that I had not taken the time to grieve. Situations like this have devastated churches in the past. Had it not been for the grace of God, this tragedy could have devastated ours. As I look back at how things turned out, I find myself asking the question, "How did we survive?" The only answer I have is God's grace. God's grace was sufficient to help us through this terrible tragedy. John Newton penned these words: "Through many dangers, toils, and snares, I have already come; Tis grace hath brought me safe thus far, and grace will lead me home."

God's Presence Leads to God's Priorities

The psalmist reminds us in Psalm 100:3 that "we are His people and the sheep of His pasture." The only person who can do whatever He wants, whenever He wants, is God. When God is allowed to sit on the throne of your life, He makes known His will for your life. We discover that our lives have value and purpose. We are not just breathing oxygen and taking up space. We discover He has a plan for our lives. Happiness and peace are experienced when we live according to His priorities.

Until we make God's priorities our priorities, we will never truly worship. The style of music you sing or how often you sing certain songs will not matter if you are not committed to God's purpose for your life. Everyone worships at some altar. Everyone in life has someone or something they worship. Some worship a hobby, job, recreation, and a lot more. They are committed to those things, and they make sacrifices to spend time with their passions. We worship at the altar of Jesus Christ. We have discovered that Jesus is all we need. In the good times and the bad times, we understand the importance of worship. Many of us have never been in a position where Jesus was all we had. We have always had something to fall back on. The early followers of Christ were placed in situations where Jesus was all they had. Each time, He was all they needed. He came through and He provided each time. When Jesus is all you have, He will be all you need.

The Bible reminds us in Deuteronomy 33:25 that "your strength will equal your days." That was God's promise to the tribe of Asher. I believe this is His promise for us today. God promises that with every need there is the right grace and strength for that need. Our problem is that we look ahead and start worrying about the strength we will need for tomorrow. God reminds us we will have tomorrow's strength when tomorrow comes. "Therefore do not worry about tomorrow, for tomorrow will worry about itself. Each day has enough trouble of its own" (Matthew 6:34).

There are things we experience in life where we do not understand how we survived. As we look back, we may still not know how we survived, but we recognize that God's grace was with us every step of the way. The strength we needed for that moment was the exact strength God provided. He knew the solution before we recognized the problem. Because God is faithful to give us strength equal to our days, we can be sure that we will not run out of strength before we run out of days. For every day we live, we can be certain there will be sufficient strength to help us through.

Worship brings us back to the center. Worship reminds us of what we were created to do. Let me encourage you to put aside the distractions in your life and focus on why you were created. Spend time worshipping God each day. Do not neglect the opportunities God gives to join with others in public worship.

Worship prepares us for the eternity that awaits us when we join with the "many angels, numbering thousands upon thousands, and ten thousands times ten thousands encircling the throne and the living creatures and the elders singing in a loud voice: Worthy is the Lamb, who was slain, to receive power and wealth and wisdom and strength and honor and glory and praise!" (Revelation 5:11–12).

Can I Give You a Boost?

3

On August 5, 2001, with the sun shining down on the historical 2.5-mile Indianapolis Motor Speedway, Jimmy Spencer and Bill Elliott led the forty-three cars to start the eighth Brickyard 400 in front of an estimated three hundred thousand people. Dave Blaney started 24th and fell toward the back with battery problems early in the race. Adding insult to injury, he also slammed into the back of Elliott Sadler's car on a restart. The front end was heavily damaged, forcing the No. 93 Dodge out of the race.

"It was all stacked up on the restart, and we took off," Blaney said. "Everybody stopped, and I ran right into the back of the No. 21. I hit him hard and tore our car up pretty bad. The battery was just going dead the whole time. We had a short in the car yesterday, and the battery went dead. The thing just wouldn't run."

Of all the NASCAR Cup races I have watched, I have only seen this happen a few times. Occasionally the car's battery loses power, and the pit crew has to replace the battery during the race. This can be very costly, because a battery cannot be replaced in the normal fifteen to eighteen second pit stop. Because the battery is located in a tight spot, it takes precious time to replace. Pit crews are very careful to make sure the batteries are fully charged before the race. There are rare exceptions when a battery is defective or loses power and must be replaced during the race. The best plan for the team is to have a fully charged battery at the beginning of each race. A fully charged battery is essential.

The problem with dead batteries is that they often die at the worst time. If you have ever tried to start your car with a dead battery, then you know how inconvenient this is. If you do not have a battery charger or another battery to boost the battery, you are likely to be late for an appointment. The sound of a fully charged battery turning over the engine is a thrill. But the clicking sound of a dead battery is rather depressing.

Do you ever feel as though your battery has gone dead in life? In the Christian race, having a fully charged battery is crucial. Nothing charges our battery for the Christian race better than fellowship.

The word *fellowship* comes from the Greek word *koinonia,* meaning "a common sharing." People having fellowship have something in common. It is more than just having something in common. Fellowship is having Jesus Christ in common. It is a word used in the Christian community to describe the type of oneness among those who know Christ as their personal Savior. A believer can have a relationship with someone who is not a believer, but they cannot have fellowship. Those who believe in Christ, and share Him in common, experience fellowship. Relationships in general can boost a person's life. Life is rather dull and boring when spent alone. But relationships are not enough for the believer. The believer requires intimate fellowship enjoyed by those who share Christ. Fellowship with other believers will boost your battery!

> With many other words he warned them; and he pleaded with them, "Save yourselves from this corrupt generation." Those who accepted his message were baptized, and about three thousand were added to their number that day. They devoted themselves to the apostles' teachings, to the fellowship, to the breaking of bread and to prayer. Everyone was filled with awe, and many wonders and miraculous signs were done by the apostles. All the believers were together and had everything in common. Selling their possessions and goods, they gave to anyone as he had need. Every day they continued to meet in the temple courts. They broke bread in their homes and ate together with glad and sincere hearts, praising God and enjoying the favor of all the people. And the Lord added to their number daily those who were being saved.
>
> —Acts 2:41–47

The New Testament believers depended on fellowship with other believers. Many were persecuted for their faith in Christ. They received strength by meeting together from house to house. They leaned on one another in difficult times. They shared possessions and goods. They spent time together. They helped support one another through prayer and Bible study. Those things proved to be invaluable and charged their batteries for the race. Fellowshipping with believers today will charge your battery for the race.

By now I hope you realize that you are running the race and you are not alone. God has provided a team of people to assist you in the race. God has put together a great pit crew to assist you with such things as worship, Bible study, and fellowship. But you must *allow* people to help. God said it was not good for man to be alone (Genesis 2:18). Man was created to have a relationship with God, as well as with his fellow man. People who share our lives assist us in the race. God's Word is the fuel that keeps us going, and worship is what brings balance to our lives, but we need other believers in order to fellowship. We can fellowship with God through prayer and the study of God's Word, but we also need to fellowship with other believers who are in fellowship with God.

"We proclaim to you what we have seen and heard, so that you also may have fellowship with us. And our fellowship is with the Father and with His Son, Jesus Christ" (1 John 1:3). The apostle John invites believers to come and enjoy the fellowship he and the other apostles enjoyed with Jesus Christ. He wrote about the life of Christ and the things he had personally witnessed Christ do while He was on the earth. The fellowship the apostles had with Christ was very special. To follow Christ around the shores of Galilee, or to sit on the side of a mountain, as He preached such life-changing words would have been awesome. Those men had front-row seats to watch the greatest person who ever lived on this earth. They did more than watch. They participated in His life. They enjoyed His fellowship, and they enjoyed the fellowship of one another. Now they are inviting us to join in this fellowship.

When a person accepts Christ as Savior, he or she becomes part of God's redeemed people. God's "redeemed" consist of believers—past, present, and future. One day God will gather all of His redeemed in one place, at one time. Everyone who has died believing in Christ, along with those professing Christ today and in the future, will be united in heaven. Just as Scripture says, "And He made known to us the mystery of His will according to His good pleasure, which He purposed in Christ, to be put into effect when the times will have reached their fulfillment—to bring all things in heaven and on earth together under one head, even Christ" (Ephesians 1:9–10).

One day we will enjoy the fellowship of every person who has accepted Christ by faith. What a day that will be! To sit down with people like Moses and Elijah will be a great experience. To talk with Peter and James without interruption will be a great joy. To talk and fellowship with many of the saints past will be a great eternity. So will the eternal time of fellowship we will enjoy with each other. There are believers I enjoy spending time with today whom I'm also looking forward to spending eternity with in heaven. I want to sit down with Moses, but I also want to sit down with some people I've shared life with today. They have been faithful friends, and I look forward to spending eternity with them. The relationships we form with other believers on earth are what we take with us to heaven. Our earthly possessions will not endure the fire that will destroy this earth one day. The relationships we have with unbelievers will not go with us to heaven. Only the fellowship we enjoy with believers we have known on earth will last forever.

The place for this fellowship today is in the Lord's church. Serving together in the Lord's church builds strong fellowship. God established His church as plan A for evangelizing the world, and there is no plan B. God expects His people to participate in His church. He equips each believer with spiritual gifts and talents in order to help support the church. Believers who are not actively involved in a local church are missing out on opportunities to fellowship. They are neither helping other believers in the race nor being supported for their own race. A racecar driver relies on assistance from the pit crew. We must learn to rely on the assistance we receive from other believers.

Each day we do the best we can to live in this world. Life can be grueling. From the schoolteacher to the student, from the car salesman to the computer programmer, people are running the race. You can only go so many laps around the track until you need a pit stop. Everything about your Christian life requires frequent service. The fuel tank runs dry; the tires need air; and eventually your battery will die. You should not wait until the battery dies to service it. Keep your battery charged by fellowshipping with other believers. Some believers wait until their batteries die before they look for help. They get busy in life and neglect the fellowship of believers, and then one day they cannot get started. They try to start their engines, but their batteries are dead.

"And let us consider how we may spur one another on toward love and good deeds. Let us not give up meeting together, as some are in the habit of doing, but let us encourage one another—and all the more as you see the Day approaching" (Hebrews 10:24–25). There is something about meeting together with other believers that inspires us. The writer of Hebrews uses the word "spur" to describe how we are to help other believers do good deeds. We must help encourage one another in the race. When we get down or discouraged, there is always someone God places in our lives to lift us up. "Two are better than one, because they have a good return for their work. If one falls down, his friend can help him up. But pity the man who falls and has no one to help him up!" (Ecclesiastes 4:9–10).

Solomon understood the importance of doing life together. Other believers encourage us in life. They help us do our best, and they inspire us to finish well. They put their arms around us and remind us that God is faithful and that with His help we can make it through the hard times. Their availability to us inspires us. We are not alone. In this way, they serve on our pit crew. We, in turn, must serve on their pit crew. Doing life together means there will be times when we need encouragement. There will be other times when we must be encouraging. If I fail in life, I sure want someone to be there to help me up. In the same way, I must be there to help others when they fail. People have often asked the question, "If I fail, will anyone care?" That's a good question and deserves an answer. But the better question is, "If someone else fails, will you care?"

"Brothers, if someone is caught in a sin, you who are spiritual should restore him gently. But watch yourself, or you also may be tempted. Carry each other's burdens, and in this way you will fulfill the law of Christ" (Galatians 6:1–2). Translated, the word "restore" in this verse is a medical term and implies setting a broken bone. When a believer fails or is caught in sin, other believers should take an interest. The believer in Galatians 6:1 was overtaken by sin. Sin caught up to him.

This person did not intend to sin. In the normal routine of life, sin caught up to him. That could happen to anyone. When a brother or sister is overtaken by sin, the spiritual believers should care and help to restore him or her in the body of Christ. No believer should be so isolated from the family of God that he or she could fall away and go unnoticed.

Life can be very difficult. As we mingle with the unbelieving world, we can run out of energy and require a boost. We receive this boost by meeting together with other believers. Life demands that we mingle with unbelievers, but we have a place where we can pull off to the side of the road and re-energize for the race. That place is the local church. The church provides us the opportunity to fellowship with other believers who experience the same hardships with the same faith. They know what it is like to run the race, and they understand the importance of healthy Christian fellowship. This is what energized the early believers, and this will energize your life as well. If you are in need of a boost today to get you back into the race, then let me suggest more frequent stops for fellowship.

The Foundation of our Fellowship

True fellowship has a foundation. "They devoted themselves to the apostles' teaching and to the fellowship" (Acts 2:42). The foundation of our fellowship is Jesus Christ. Every believer does not believe everything the same. There are some fundamental things believed by all believers. There are some things we do not believe the same. The fundamental things we all believe include salvation by grace through faith, the bodily resurrection of Jesus Christ, the virgin birth, and the second coming of Christ. Those fundamentals form the basis of our fellowship in Christ. Negotiable issues include whether or not Christ will come back before, during, or after the tribulation; should believers drink alcohol; and the translation of the Bible you use. Those issues and others form the basis of our fellowship with one another. Many of these points divide Christianity into different denominations. In heaven, all the denominational tags will be removed, but on earth, they create an atmosphere of peace. Those with a strong doctrinal position on an issue find it difficult to attend a church where that issue is taught differently. Howard Conway, a mentor, once told me, "There are things in life that you will die for. There are other things that you will fight for, and there are some things that you will argue about. The wise man does not die over something barely worth an argument."

"The apostles' teaching" formed the foundation of the early church's fellowship. They disagreed on some things, but they agreed that Jesus Christ is Lord. They worked through their differences. They discovered that doctrine does matter. What we believe forms the foundation of our fellowship. You should study the Scriptures and attend a church that teaches the Bible accurately. Some insist doctrine does *not* matter. They believe that all of God's people should be able to worship together and get along, regardless of what they believe. That will happen in heaven, but is not likely to happen on earth. We are not as informed in the present as we will be in heaven. All of us will have our eyes enlightened in heaven.

Doctrine matters because it's part of what determines a person's behavior. How a person acts will be the result of what he or she believes. Some take the reverse approach and allow their behavior to determine what they believe (2 Timothy 4:3–4). If you want to finish the race well, you must determine your behavior from what you believe, as long as what you believe is consistent with truth. The truth sets a person free, so long as they live by the truth. The same truth that frees one may condemn another.

The apostle Paul told the believers in the church at Corinth that they needed to agree to disagree about meat sacrificed in idol worship (1 Corinthians 8:1–13). There were some in the church who believed believers should not purchase meat in the market from an animal that had been sacrificed to an idol god. Others felt this was permissible, because the idol did not exist anyway. If a person could buy the meat at a discount price, they considered this as being a good steward of their money. That debate was dividing some in the church in Corinth. The apostle Paul told them not to force their opinions on each other. Agree to disagree and move on.

There will be issues that divide. Try not to be divisive. Try to find common ground with believers so you can enjoy Christian fellowship. If you want to be charged for the race, then build relationships with believers who share your interpretation of Scripture, and try to be a little more tolerant of those who see things differently.

The Fruit of our Fellowship

Once again we return to the early church for our model. "All the believers were together and had everything in common" (Acts 2:44). Do you think that is correct? Could they really have everything in common? They had *enough* in common. They had Jesus Christ in common. They made a decision to follow Jesus and to make Him the Lord of their lives. For many this meant persecution and death. Jesus once said that the Father would separate out from the world His followers. That separation made them so different from the world that they did not recognize any differences with one another. We should not assume that the early believers did not disagree on issues. They had many disagreements documented in the written accounts, but they remained on track. They submitted to the Holy Spirit as their guide and companion. They were faithfully following one head, Jesus Christ. Rather than allowing their disagreements to divide, they used them to further the gospel.

> Some time later Paul said to Barnabas, "Let us go back and visit the brothers in all towns where we preached the word of the Lord and see how they are doing." Barnabas wanted to take John, also called Mark, with them, but Paul did not think it wise to take him, because he had deserted them in Pamphylia and had not continued with them in the work. They had such sharp disagreement that they parted company. Barnabas took Mark and sailed for Cyprus, but Paul chose Silas and left, commended by the brothers to the grace of the Lord.
>
> —Acts 15:36–40

There was sharp disagreement between Paul and Barnabas over Mark. The two could not come to an agreement about Mark, so they both took someone different. Rather than the gospel having one missionary team, it now had two missionary teams. Their disagreement produced a positive result for the gospel. The two men agreed to disagree and moved on. Later, Paul would change his opinion about Mark. "Get

Mark and bring him with you, because he is helpful to me in my ministry" (2 Timothy 4:11). Barnabas believed in Mark much the same way he believed in Paul. Barnabas was the one who encouraged the church to accept Paul and who would later accompany him on his missionary trips. Barnabas is the kind of Christian man I want on my pit crew in life.

The fellowship of the early believers produced unity. The fact they had everything in common implies that they shared the same main purpose. The priority of the early church was to preach the gospel and declare to the world the resurrection of Jesus Christ. They were focused on this purpose and did not allow other issues to distract them. When other issues occurred, the believers quickly appointed people to handle them so they could stay on track. I have an entire chapter devoted to distractions in this book. Being distracted can greatly affect how we finish the race.

Being distracted by good things can cause a church to lose focus, resulting in poor fellowship among the believers. A church that loses purpose will lose unity. People unite for a purpose. People are also divided when there is no clear purpose. The strength of the early church was that they knew where they were going, exactly what they were doing, and how they planned to get there. Good fellowship in a church will lead to unity of purpose, but that unity is actually produced by the Holy Spirit. Good fellowship creates the right atmosphere for the Spirit's unity. "Make every effort to keep the unity of the Spirit through the bond of peace" (Ephesians 4:3). While believers do not create unity, they have everything to do with unity remaining in the church.

An attitude of giving was also produced by the fellowship of the early believers. "Selling their possessions and goods, they gave to anyone as he had need" (Acts 2:45). Because they had Christ in common, they assisted one another with the necessities of life. The early believers experienced persecution in many forms. Some were denied jobs. They were unable to support their families. They were not allowed to work. They were denied work, so other believers gave assistance. This giving attitude and concern for one another made for a dynamic atmosphere in the early church. No wonder they grew so rapidly and had God's blessings upon them. People will beat a path to the door of a church where they are loved and accepted.

The Force of our Fellowship

The fellowship of the early believers had an inward and outward effect. Inwardly, the Scripture says, "everyone was filled with awe" (Acts 2:43), and outwardly it says, "the Lord added to their number daily those who were being saved" (Acts 2:47). Where God works, there will be a new respect for righteousness. When believers submit to God as a group, together they can be agents of change. The early church was reported as having "turned the world upside down" (Acts 17:6). They influenced the world rather than being influenced by the world. The first-century world had to sit up and take notice of those untrained and unschooled men. The early believers understood God was working through them. They did not take credit for what God was doing. They were filled with awe. A sense of awe and respect is brought to our lives today when we realize that God is working through us.

This sense of internal respect that we have is contagious and will cause others to believe in our God. The people of the world observe the fellowship we enjoy with other believers. They are looking for deeper relationships in life. They want something real and deeper than the surface relationships that exist most of the time in society. They want to be with people who have all things in common and who are willing to help them in the race. The early church grew so rapidly because the Holy Spirit was working powerfully through their fellowship. They were ridiculed and persecuted in life, but they found comfort and strength in being with one another. They met often, and their meetings energized them to finish the race.

You may be running the race so fast today that you have failed to check the battery. You may think charging your battery will take too much of your time. If you avoid the warning signs, you are likely to be knocked out of the race. There are usually signs to tell you a battery is losing its power, but you have to pay attention. There are also signs in life to warn us that we need a boost.

If you have become apathetic toward spiritual things, or critical, this could be an indication that your battery needs a boost. If the spiritual fire has gone out of your life, then you likely are in need of a boost.

The best way to boost your battery is to enjoy the fellowship God has provided for you through the pit crew that surrounds your life in a local church.

Talk to Your Chief

4

Tight quarters and a slippery track made for tough going at the 2002 CMT 300 at the New Hampshire International Speedway, but Jeff Gordon took the lead with a fuel-only pit stop on Lap 228 and held it for his 10th Cup victory of the season.

Gordon was having radio trouble with his crew and didn't get the word until the last second to come in. Ernie Irvan was taking on two new tires, so Gordon's crew chief, Ray Evernham, chose to take fuel only and get off pit row fast.

"I felt like the only way he could beat (Irvan) was if we got track position and hope he got in traffic," Evernham said. "It all worked out. We kind of gambled on the win, and ended up winning."

Stress is a common factor for many in America. People often discuss the stress that is in their lives. Stress is everywhere. Some are stressed at home because of financial or family issues. Others are stressed at work because of demanding jobs. Many are stressed by health concerns. Stress is a major problem in our country. God has an answer for stress. God's answer for stress is called prayer.

"You will keep in perfect peace him whose mind is steadfast, because he trusts in you" (Isaiah 26:3).

Some of the most stressful jobs in American are those of airline pilots, air traffic controllers, astronauts, and NASCAR drivers. The pilot and air traffic controller have hundreds of lives depending on them to make the right decision at the right time. Blasting off into outer space and re-entering the earth's atmosphere, in a machine protected from scalding temperatures by a thin layer of insulated panels, is very stressful. Driving an automobile at speeds up to 200 miles an hour, around a two and one-half mile track, with forty-two other cars, can be very stressful. There is one thing all of these people have in common. Each one has someone to talk with on the other end of a radio. Pilots talk to the air traffic controller. Astronauts talk to the technicians at NASA. The racer talks to the crew chief on pit row.

You and I can talk with God as we run the Christian race. Through prayer, we are in constant communication with the one who knows everything that will happen to us in the race. NASCAR teams communicate with one another by radio. The entire team communicates with each other during the race. The spotter communicates information to the driver. The crew communicates with the crew chief. The driver communicates with the pit crew, and the crew chief communicates with the driver. All the information is assimilated by the crew chief in order for him to direct the driver. The crew chief is the most informed on the team. He is the one best equipped to direct the driver. When the driver communicates with the crew chief, he understands he is speaking to the one in charge.

As we turn to God in prayer, we understand we are submitting to the one in charge of our lives. Prayer is absolutely essential to running an effective race. If you expect to run well, you must learn the importance of prayer. If you neglect prayer in your Christian life, you are neglecting one of the greatest privileges you have received from God. The opportunity to talk to our Heavenly Father at any time and any place is a tremendous privilege. Most believers will admit they do not pray often enough. Prayer reminds us we are not alone in the race. You may feel lonely at times, but you are never alone. God is as close as a prayer. If your life is filled with stress and you feel like you are being squeezed in by the traffic around you, I want to encourage you to talk to your chief.

Sometimes the most profound words are the simplest words. Paul wrote in Romans 12:12, "Be joyful in hope, patient in affliction, faithful in prayer." Those three phrases of instruction would be good advice for a racecar driver. Every racecar driver would do well to practice those three things. So would you. You need the joy that comes from having hope in Jesus Christ. During times of affliction, we must persevere and not give up. If we plan to finish the race well, we must be faithful in prayer.

All during the race, the driver communicates with the crew chief. That reminds me of the words Paul wrote in 1 Thessalonians 5:17:

"Pray continually." Is that really possible? Can we talk to God all the time? The answer is yes. You and I can live in such a way that we are in constant communication with God. Every minute of every day we are free to talk with God. As our companion in life, God wants to be included.

"While they were worshiping the Lord and fasting, the Holy Spirit said, 'Set apart for me Barnabas and Saul for the work to which I have called them'" (Acts 13:2).

The relationship between the early church and the Holy Spirit was such that the church heard Him speak. He was one with them. The Holy Spirit was involved in their decisions. As the early church was worshipping, the Holy Spirit spoke to them about sending out the first missionaries. When Barnabas and Saul went on their first missionary journey, they took the Holy Spirit with them. Their journey was a partnership between them and the Holy Spirit. The relationship was so real that the apostles spoke to Him and He spoke to the apostles. Your relationship with the Holy Spirit should be no different. Many times we allow our relationship with God to be interrupted. We are not communicating with Him.

The book of Daniel records an interesting story. The Babylonians, around 605 B.C., took Daniel, Hananiah, Misheal, and Azariah captive. They were very young Hebrew men at the time, but they proved to be faithful to God by standing for their convictions. They refused to eat the royal food and wine set before them. They offered a test between them and the other young men King Nebuchadnezzar was training to enter the king's service. At the end of ten days, they looked healthier and better nourished than any of the young men who ate the royal food. The king gave those young Hebrews special privileges. He placed them in positions of authority in Babylon. Daniel became gifted at interpreting dreams. He was used of God to influence King Nebuchadnezzar.

Daniel had distinguished himself among the administrators and satraps by his exceptional qualities. The king planned to set him over the whole kingdom. That infuriated the other administrators and satraps. They decided to set a trap for Daniel. The only problem was that they could not find any corruption in Daniel. Here is what they concluded:

"We will never find any basis for charges against this man Daniel unless it has something to do with the law of his God" (Daniel 6:5).

Those enemies of Daniel went to the king with a proposal. They knew Daniel was a man of prayer. He prayed three times a day. They proposed to the king that he establish himself as the only Supreme Being. They suggested he issue a decree that anyone caught praying, in the next thirty days, to another god or man should be thrown into the lion's den. That pleased the king, and he signed the order into law. Notice what Daniel did: "Now when Daniel learned that the decree had been published, he went home to his upstairs room where the windows opened toward Jerusalem. Three times a day he got down on his knees and prayed, giving thanks to his God, just as he had done before" (Daniel 6:10).

Many things impress me about this verse, but what impresses me the most is the phrase, "where the windows opened toward Jerusalem." Often we have to spend time opening our windows in order to talk with God. When the window is already open, you can begin praying. That is what Daniel did. He was able to pray because his window was already open. Daniel was not trying to be defiant by praying three times a day. He already prayed three times a day. The king's decree would not stop Daniel from praying to his God.

When my wife, Ann, and I rented our first house, it required a lot of work. We lived in an apartment for the first six months of our marriage. We were so glad to move into a house. Even though we were just renting, the house was so much better than living in an apartment. Like most newlyweds, we did not have a lot of money. We could not afford to buy a home or to pay much in rent. When the landlord said we could paint the house for the deposit, we were all over that! I will never forget trying to raise the windows in that house. We cut away layers of caulking and paint just so we could raise the windows enough to allow the fumes from the paint to escape. Raising those windows was not easy and required a lot of time and effort.

Many of us have found that our window to heaven has been caulked and painted so much that we have a difficult time raising it to pray. Maybe you need to talk to God but your window to heaven is stuck. You have painted around the window in order to make it look attractive, but the paint is getting in the way. The lack of any real prayer life has been camouflaged by a lot of decorative paint. There may be times in your life when you can wait on God. You may have plenty of time to spend with God and get things right before you need His help. There will be other times when you will find yourself like Simon Peter. He was walking on the water, but he began to sink. There was no time for Peter to raise his window. Peter needed a direct line of communication with Jesus. He didn't have time to use long words and small talk. He only had time to pray: "Lord, save me!" (Matthew 14:30). The Lord heard Simon's prayer and helped him back into the boat.

When a NASCAR driver speaks to his crew chief, he wants to know that the radio is working. You need to realize that if you are not getting through to God, the problem is not that prayer does not work; the problem is that you are not praying. You can talk to God anytime and anyplace. You can talk to God about any and everything happening in your life. He wants us to pray. He invites us to pray. Jesus even taught us how to pray: "This, then, is how you should pray: 'Our Father in heaven, hallowed be your name, your kingdom come, your will be done on earth as it is in heaven. Give us today our daily bread. Forgive us our debts, as we also have forgiven our debtors. And lead us not into temptation, but deliver us from the evil one'" (Matthew 6:9–13).

The apostles were so impressed by the way Jesus prayed that they once said, "Lord, teach us to pray" (Luke 11:1). There is no written account where they ever asked Jesus to teach them to preach or to do miracles. They did, however, ask Him to teach them to pray.

God wants to be the kind of partner in your life whom you will share things with. He wants to walk and talk with you every day. He enjoys spending time with you. God has always wanted to be with His people. In the Old Testament, God was present with Israel in the Tabernacle. Later in the Temple, He resided between the Cherubim over the Mercy Seat in the Holy of Holies. In the New Testament, God dwelt with His people in the person of Jesus Christ. Today God is present with us as His Spirit lives in each believer. You do not have to know certain words to communicate with God. You can pray to God in the same way you would talk to a friend. Each time you do, you will find He will hear you and is aware of what is happening in your life. He has all the facts. You have just a few. You see the traffic near you, but God sees everything on the track. He can help you watch out for things that will distract or hurt you in the race. He also knows what is going on in your life. He knows when you need a pit stop.

Prayer Brings Peace

Very few words are as calming as when someone says, "Let us pray!" As a pastor, I can tell you that those words can bring peace to a person's life. Many times I have been in a hospital room with a family just receiving bad news. When I asked if I could pray for them, their hearts were set at peace. I have been at the graveside as family members said their final good-byes. I have watched peace prevail when we prayed. Prayer brings peace to our troubled souls unlike anything else. Prayer reassures our minds that God is listening. God cares! God can help!

Stephen found peace through prayer when he was being stoned. "While they were stoning him, Stephen prayed, 'Lord Jesus, receive my spirit.' Then he fell on his knees and cried out, 'Lord, do not hold this sin against them.' When he had said this, he fell asleep" (Acts 7:59). In spite of the chaos, and above the yelling of the mob, he discovered God's peace. He was okay with dying. He even found grace in his heart to forgive the people stoning him. Prayer can do amazing things for your attitude. Evidently, Stephen accepted this as his time to die. When he looked up, he saw Jesus standing to receive him as he died. Prayer brings peace, because we discover God's will through prayer. There is no greater peace than knowing you are in God's will. God's will is not always the safest place. Many times, God will lead us into unsafe places. In the story mentioned above, in Matthew, chapter 14, when Peter walked on the water, Jesus was the one who directed the apostles to go into that storm. They didn't know they would soon be in a storm, but Jesus certainly did.

God's will may not be the safest place, but it is the most peaceful. You can have peace in the storm if you are where God wants you to be. Being in an unsafe place in God's will is better than being in the safest place outside the will of God. When God guides, God provides. Where God leads, He intercedes. While the apostles were in the storm of their lives, Jesus was on the mountain praying. I assume He was praying for them. He often did pray for them. Sometimes the will of God will lead you into places that you may not want to go. A little boy came to a Scout meeting late one day, and his Scout Master asked him, "Why are you late?" The little boy replied, "I was helping a woman cross the street." The Scout Master asked, "Why did that take so long?" The little boy replied, "She didn't want to go."

I feel like that woman sometimes. God is taking me places where I really do not want to go. I would rather not be in the situation where God has led me. When we surrender to His will and accept that He knows best, we will experience peace. Nothing is as wonderful as peace. Surrender and obedience to God's will come most often through prayer. Maybe you need to turn something over to God right now. Perhaps you have been carrying a burden, or perhaps you have felt unrest about where you are in life, only to realize that your crew chief has guided you every step of the way. Rather than argue with God about the circumstance, I encourage you to submit to God. You will discover His peace. Remember, you do not have all the information that God has about your surroundings. God is aware of the pitfalls Satan has waiting for you. Talk to God. Discover His peace.

A racecar driver has to trust the crew chief. He has to accept the fact that the chief knows more about what is happening than he does. When he releases everything to the chief, the driver can enjoy the race. Many are not enjoying the race as believers. They argue with God over what is the best way to go or the best thing to do rather than trust Him. When you pray, you are putting your trust in God. The best way to live a peaceful and happy life is to live in obedient trust to God. You are at your best when you are trusting. God is at His best when He is trusted.

Prayer Brings Power

There is power in prayer!

Prayer changes things!

These are both statements believers often make about prayer. There are two things to keep in mind. First, prayer itself is not the power. Power comes from God, who answers our prayers. When we pray, we tap into what God can do. God can do anything. Through prayer, you get beyond what *you* can do, and you receive the added power from *God*. Secondly, prayer changes *us* more than prayer changes *things*. Through prayer, we learn to submit to God's will about things. The Son of God prayed in the Garden: "My Father, if it is possible, may this cup be taken from me. Yet not as I will, but as you will" (Matthew 26:39).

God answers every prayer. Sometimes God answers yes; sometimes God answers no. Sometimes God tells us to wait. We would prefer God answer yes every time to our prayers. But because God knows what He is doing in our lives and how our lives fit into His plan, He always answers correctly. By accepting God's will for your life rather than arguing with God about the answer, you will gain greater power in your life. God changes things, but He uses our prayers to change things by changing us. As we discern God's will through prayer and release our will to His will, we receive God's peace. Jesus wrestled in the garden about the cross. He agonized over those three hours when the Father would turn His back on the Son. This was not the way Jesus wanted things, but ultimately, He surrendered to the Father's will. That gave Him the power to face the trial, the rejection of the people, and the crucifixion for which He was destined.

Prayer that is surrendered to the Father will result in power. When our asking corresponds with the Father's will to give, we can expect to receive answered prayers. Many times the things we ask from God are out of His will to give us. "When you ask, you do not receive, because you ask with wrong motives, that you may spend what you get on your pleasures" (James 4:3).

When you surrender to God's will, you are not likely to ask for things outside of God's will. If you ask for something that God has already determined to give you, then you can expect to receive what you asked for. But if you are asking for things God has no intention of giving you, then you are obviously out of touch with God's will for your life. The first step to receiving answered prayer is to be in harmony with God. When your will and God's will are the same for your life, then you are more likely to know what to ask for, and God will give it to you because it is part of His plan for your life. He already planned to give it to you anyway.

There was a businessman who was also a widower. He was raising two young boys on his own. His job required that he travel frequently, but he always brought something, from the places he traveled, home to his sons after each trip. On one occasion he did not bring anything home, but instead took his two sons shopping. He told them they could buy anything they wanted if they saw it in the store. As they entered the store, the first thing they saw was candy. They asked their father if they could have some candy. He said they could if they really wanted the candy, but he wanted them to walk around some more to make sure the candy was really what they wanted. As they walked around the store they repeated the same scene. They would see something they really wanted, ask their father for it, and he would suggest they walk around some more to make sure. Finally, as they came to the back of the store, they found the bicycles. They looked up at their father and asked, "Dad, can we have two bicycles?" The father replied, "That is what I brought you here to buy." We are just like those boys with God. We ask for everything we see, until finally we ask for what God the Father wants to give us.

When you get in harmony with His will for your life, you learn to ask for the things God intends to give you. You also learn what not to ask for. You are in agreement with God that He knows best.

Another important ingredient to powerful prayer is faith. "If you believe, you will receive whatever you ask for in prayer" (Matthew 21:22).

Jesus emphasized the importance of faith throughout His life. He encouraged people to believe in Him and to believe in the Father. All prayer is an act of faith, because the person who prays believes in someone he or she does not see. God honors faith. He honors prayer offered in faith, because faith pleases Him. The only way to come to God is by faith. "And without faith it is impossible to please God, because anyone who comes to him must believe that he exists and that he rewards those who earnestly seek him" (Hebrews 11:6).

God not only honors faith, but also He blesses our faith. Faith is what moves God to move things. He is more impressed with our acting out of faith than He is with what we actually do. God will not bless works that are not generated by faith. The fact that you attend church weekly is not what impresses Him. The fact that you believe in God enough to attend church each week is what pleases Him. The fact you may tithe out of your income to the church is not what impresses God. The fact that you believe in Him enough to give ten percent of your income to the Lord is what pleases Him. The same is true when we pray. You need something and you have enough faith in God to ask Him. That is what pleases God. Faith is not a credit card that allows us to ask for anything we want. Faith is what leads us to bring our request to God, knowing that He can do something about our situation. He can change the things that are happening. He can intervene and make the result different. I believe He can, and when by faith I come asking, He does.

There is one more ingredient to powerful prayer. We are told to ask in Jesus name. "And I will do whatever you ask in my name, so that the Son may bring glory to the Father" (John 14:13).

Many have taken this to mean that as long as we use Jesus' name when we pray, we are entitled to everything we ask for. When Jesus spoke about using His name, He meant more than closing our prayers with the words, "in Jesus name." Before Jesus died on the cross, access to the Father was through sacrifices offered at the Temple. When Jesus died on the cross, the veil of the Temple was ripped from top to bottom. That was miraculous and one of several phenomena that occurred that day. The ripping of the veil was more than something caused by a natural disaster, however. The ripping of the veil was a statement from God declaring that access to the Father was no longer through animal sacrifices. Access to God was now through His Son, Jesus Christ. "For there is one God and one mediator between God and men, the man Christ Jesus" (1 Timothy 2:5).

The only way to the Father is through faith in His Son. The only prayer that God hears today is prayer that is offered in faith through Jesus Christ. Those who do not have faith in Christ do not have the ear of the Heavenly Father. The first prayer of the unbeliever must be the sinner's prayer, when he or she calls on Christ for salvation (Romans 10:9–13). Praying in Jesus' name means that you believe Jesus Christ is the Son of God and the only way to heaven. Prayer, in Jesus' name, means you have come to Him by faith and accepted His death on the cross as payment for your sin. God placed you into the Kingdom of

His Son. Because you are in His Son, He hears you when you pray (John 15:7).

My aunt, Georgia Hogan, was a devoted follower of Christ. She loved to write poetry, and many of her poems reflect her walk with God. I was touched by this poem she wrote that was read at her memorial service.

On the Wings of Prayer

Just close your eyes
and open your heart
And feel your worries
and cares depart,
Just yield yourself
to the Father above
And let him hold you
secure in his love—
For life on Earth
grows more involved
With endless problems
that can't be solved
But God only asks us
to do our best,
Then He will take over
and finish the rest
So when you are tired,
discouraged, and blue,
There's always one door
that is open to you
And that is the door
to "The House of Prayer"
And you'll find God waiting
to meet you there,
And the House of Prayer
is no farther away
Than the quiet spot
where you kneel and pray—

For the heart is a temple
when God is there
As we place ourselves
in his loving care,
And He heard every prayer
and answers each one
When we pray in His name
"Thy will be done"
And the burdens that seemed
too heavy to bear
Are lifted away
On "The Wings of Prayer"

Prayer Brings Potential

There is no limit to God's power or to what He can do. Through prayer, we tap into God's power. When you trust a bank, you get what money can do. When you trust a doctor, you get what medicine can do. But when you trust God, you get what God can do, which is unlike anything anyone else can do.

I believe God expects us to be persistent in prayer:

> Suppose one of you has a friend, and he goes to him at midnight and says, "Friend, lend me three loaves of bread, because a friend of mine on a journey has come to me, and I have nothing to set before him." Then the one inside answers, "Don't bother me, the door is already locked, and my children are with me in bed. I can't get up and give you anything." I tell you, though he will not get up and give him the bread because he is his friend, yet because of the man's boldness he will get up and give him as much as he needs. So I say to you: Ask and it will be given to you, seek and you will find, knock and the door will be opened to you. For everyone who asks receives; he who seeks finds; and to him who knocks, the door will be open.
>
> —Luke 11:5–10

Jesus taught that those who ask and keep on asking will get what they ask for. The one who seeks and continues to seek finds what he or she is looking for. The one who knocks and keeps on knocking is bound to receive an open door. The man in Jesus' story did not want to get up to give his friend the food because he did not want to wake up his children. If you have ever tried to get small children to go back to bed after they have been awakened, then you can understand this man's situation. Because his friend continued to persist, however, the man did answer the door. How many times have you given up on prayer too soon? Maybe God was about to give you what you were asking for, but you were not persistent enough to keep asking. There is a difference between when God says "no" and when God says "wait." Perhaps God is asking you to wait a little longer so you can continue to ask, seek, or knock. Anything worth having is worth being persistent for.

You must also remain patient when you pray. God is not on our clock. He does not always do things according to our timetable. The Christian is like a farmer who prepares the ground, plants the seed, but then must wait for the rain. The farmer cannot control the rain. The farmer can only prepare the soil and plant the seed. God sends the rain. The farmer can only do so much. He must wait on God. The people of Israel lived in Egypt for over four hundred years, waiting for God to send a deliverer. They cried out for God to help. Then one day God sent Moses. The hardest thing is to leave things in God's hands. We give things to God, but we grow impatient and take them back again. We think God is not handling things well enough, so we take them back. One of my favorite slogans is, "Never dig up in doubt what you have laid down in faith." God heard the cries of Israel, and He hears your cries for help today.

There are many people who can and will assist you in the race, but the one in charge is God. He is the crew chief, and He must be the one in control of your life. He calls the shots. He tells you when the time has come to make a stop and when you need to keep moving. Stay in communication with Him. Talk to Him every day. If possible, talk to Him throughout the day. He has the answers. He knows the plan He has for your life.

Listen to Your Spotter

5

At the 2005 Sony HDTV 500 at the California Speedway, Dale Earnhardt Jr. took the lead for two laps after the rest of the field pitted on lap 200. Earnhardt Jr. pitted on lap 203, in an attempt to stretch the fuel mileage to the end of the race, but fuel economy became a moot issue on lap 211 when the engine disintegrated in a dramatic and smoky end to the evening. The late afternoon starting time presented visibility problems for the drivers, who were forced to look directly into the setting sun along the backstretch and into Turn Three. Earnhardt Jr. spoke up about the problem during a yellow-flag period on lap 94.

Earnhardt Jr. (speaking to spotter Jimmie Kitchens): "I can't see a thing on the backstretch." Spotter—"I'm really concerned about going into Turn Three with someone on my right corner. I'm concerned about that because I could drive right into them. So just stay on the radio all the way through the corner if someone's out there. It's not going to bother me if you just keep talking all the way through the corners. Just stay on the radio."

If you have ever driven a car, then you are probably aware of the term "blind spots." Blind spots are places around the automobile where you cannot see directly ahead of you, or on the sides and behind you by looking in one of the mirrors. In order to see, you have to actually turn your head and look directly at the spot(s) in question. Objects may not appear in the mirrors, but they are there. Drivers are taught in safety courses to turn their heads and look at the blind spots before changing lanes or making sudden turns.

In a NASCAR race, there are blind spots for the drivers. With forty-two other cars driving at speeds up to 200 miles an hour, the amazing thing is that more accidents do not occur. How do the drivers keep from running into each other all the time? The answer is that every driver has a spotter who stands at the top of the racetrack and radios information to the driver about the other vehicles that will help guide the driver around traffic.

God has provided the equivalent of a spotter for us. He understands that in the race of life there are blind spots. Everyone has things in their lives that are detrimental to their walks with God. We cannot see them. We have a responsibility to help each other with things we cannot see alone. Jesus addressed this subject in the Sermon on the Mount. "Why do you look at the speck of sawdust in your brother's eye and pay no attention to the plank in your own eye? How can you say to your brother, 'Let me take the speck out of your eye,' when all the time there is a plank in your own eye? You hypocrite, first take the plank out of your own eye, and then you will see clearly to remove the speck from your brother's eye" (Matthew 7:3–5).

At the end of verse five, Jesus said, "Then you will see clearly." Jesus did not forbid judging. He taught that the proper way to help someone else with his or her faults is to begin with our own faults. Once you have been honest about your own faults and have confessed them before God, you are ready to assist other believers because you can see more clearly. Every believer needs a spotter. We need someone who can see the things we cannot because we are too close to our own situation. Mature believers who have a bird's eye view of our lives can be a tremendous help to us in the race. Everyone should be accountable to someone in life. Ultimately, we are all accountable to God. One day we will stand before God in judgment. Having someone in life who holds us accountable will make that judgment less intimidating. If we will honestly deal with the issues happening in our lives today, then perhaps we can avoid repeating them in the future.

The subject of accountability is uncomfortable to some. The idea of allowing someone to become so close to us that they can speak to us about personal issues frightens many in the faith. James was the half brother of Jesus. He wrote, "Confess your sins to each other" (James 5:16). James understood the importance of having someone in your life share your weaknesses and hold you accountable. I heard a story about a man who struggled with lust in his life. He had recently become a believer and learned about the importance of having an accountability partner in life. He was out of town on business, and a group of men invited him to go out on the town with them. He hesitated about going but decided he would go in order to be with the guys. Then he picked up the phone and called his accountability partner back home and said, "I want you to call me at 6:00 A.M. and ask me what I did last night."

If you are not enrolled in an accountability group somewhere, you are doing a disservice to your Christian life. Acknowledging your faults is not a sign of weakness, but rather a sign of maturity. No one is exempt from having blind spots. There is nothing weak about admitting you struggle in certain areas of your life. You are not likely to defeat your struggles until you own them and ask someone to help you.

One of the longest running television shows was Gunsmoke. Marshall Dillon protected a lot of people and upheld law and order in Dodge City for over twenty years. I remember an episode once where Matt Dillon was asked to come and help a neighboring town with a crime wave. The sheriff in town was an old friend but had become an alcoholic. It was just going to be him and Matt Dillon against the wave of crime that had made it into town because of the sheriff's alcoholism. Matt tried everything to shock his friend back into his old self, but the man ultimately decided that he would have to kick the habit alone. That night he sat at the table with an open bottle of whiskey and stared at it all night. He fought the temptation. He wiped his lips many times. He opened the bottle. He poured drinks. He held the bottle to his lips, but he never took a drink. By morning he had kicked his habit.

That may work in Hollywood, but is not likely in real life. Many believers have tried to stand against temptation like that sheriff. They think they are alone. God wants you to know that you are not alone. God is with you, but He also has placed people in your life to help you.

Ultimately, you must resist the temptation. No one can do that for you. You are the one who will have to make the choice to stop or to lay certain things aside in your life, but other people can help hold you accountable. If you do not tell anyone or allow someone you trust to speak to you openly and honestly, you may not know the damage that is being done to your life. In the book of Galatians, chapter 6, there are two conflicting statements. In verse two, the apostle Paul wrote, "Carry each other's burdens, and in this way you will fulfill the law of Christ." Then he writes in verse five, "Each one should carry his own load."

Those two verses seem to conflict. In verse two, he writes that we should help each other with burdens, but in verse five he writes that we should carry our own load. Both statements are accurate because there are things in life that no one can help us carry. They can support us in prayer and be an encourager while we are carrying the load, but they cannot help us. This load is one we must carry alone. There are other times when people can assist us. They can offer more than a prayer and words of encouragement. They can actually help us carry the load.

After my son was married, he and his new wife, Amy, moved into an apartment. He and I were moving some mattresses they'd purchased up to their third-floor apartment. The stairs curved so you had to go up halfway and then make a sharp right turn. On the same day we were moving those mattresses, the appliance store had sent a crew to deliver my son and daughter-in-law's new washer and dryer. We'd been struggling to carry those mattresses up the stairs and had made it to the halfway point, between the second and third floor, while the two-man appliance crew went ahead of us. All of a sudden, like hands from heaven reaching over the railing of the balcony, those two men lifted the mattress to the third floor. My son, Jared, and I broke into the "Hallelujah Chorus." The men delivering the washer and dryer had become tired of waiting for us to clear the staircase and decided to help. We thought we'd have to carry the burden alone, but on that day there were two men to help.

The same is true in your life. There will be times when you will have to go through some things alone. As much as a friend or family member would like to help, there will be nothing they can do. They will uphold you in prayer and be ready to assist you when the time comes, but the burden is not one they can remove. But most burdens in life *can* be shared, and when temptation and dealing with the trials of life come, God has given you help. He has provided other believers in this life to help us identify our "blind spots." More importantly, He has placed you in the life of someone else so you can help him or her with "blind spots." To be a good spotter, we must understand Jesus' words in Matthew 7:3–5, and remove the plank out of our own life so that we can see clearly the speck in our brother's eye. This speaks to three very important issues: who to judge, when to judge, and how to judge.

Who to Judge

Before you can assist someone with his or her "blind spots," you must first deal with your own "blind spots." That is what Jesus meant in Matthew 7:3. In Matthew 7:2 Jesus said, "For in the same way you judge others, you will be judged, and with the measure you use, it will be measured to you." People are most likely to be critical of things in others that exist in their own lives. For some reason, sin always appears worse in another person than in us. We may be guilty of the same thing we criticize in someone else, but the issue does not appear to be as magnified in our lives as in theirs. Perhaps the reason we judge the same thing in others is to draw the attention away from ourselves. This does not excuse the sin in the life of our brothers and sisters, but it means that before we can help him or her, we must deal with those same issues ourselves. My brother needs help, but I cannot possibly benefit him until I deal with my own faults.

One way the Lord taught us to judge ourselves is at the Lord's Table. The Lord's Supper is an examination meal. "A man ought to examine himself before he eats of the bread and drinks of the cup. For anyone who eats and drinks without recognizing the body of the Lord eats and drinks judgment on himself. That is why many among you are weak and sick, and a number of you have fallen asleep. But if we judge ourselves, we would not come under judgment" (1 Corinthians 11:28–31).

There is something humbling about holding in our hands the bread and cup that reminds us of the body and blood of our Savior. Taking the Lord's Supper makes you want to examine your life. When you consider the price Jesus paid for you to have eternal life, you want to stop and evaluate everything happening in your life. The Lord understands that each believer has an internal witness to help bring conviction for sin. Conviction is God's way of helping us to identify our sin so we can repent of our sin and receive His forgiveness. There is a difference between conviction and guilt. Guilt is something Satan uses to lead us deeper into sin. Conviction is how the Holy Spirit leads us out of sin.

Conflict is another method God uses to help us judge ourselves. Conflict in our lives is God's way of drawing attention to some areas we have neglected. Blaming someone else is easy when you have conflict. But God wants us to understand that conflict is His way of drawing attention to things we cannot see. A lot of people read with a highlight marker. As they read, they highlight certain sentences or paragraphs. That way, when they read the book again or skim the book for highlights they will notice the highlighted portions. Those are the things they want to remember or to take note of from their reading. In the same way, God wants to highlight issues in our lives that need our attention. The most effective way for God to highlight them is to draw our attention through conflict or the trials of life. He is not sending these trials in order to make us miserable. He is drawing attention to issues in our lives. As we deal with these issues, we will be happier. God wants to cut away everything in our lives that does not remind Him of Jesus Christ. In order to cut away things such as pride and lust, He must expose these things. He uses conflict in our lives, as well as trials and tribulations, to expose them.

A few years back I went through a very painful period of time. Even though I have been the pastor of Fellowship Baptist Church in Forney, Texas for thirty years, there have been times when it would have been easier to leave than to stay. There was a time when I was intimidated by opposition. I thought when people questioned my leadership they were acting carnal and needed to get right with God. I have learned over the years that I am not always right. People have opinions that matter to them, and I have to guard against pride. Conflict with an elder, deacon, church member, or even guests can lead me to act prideful. God has shown me how much He hates pride and how much work I have to do to remove pride from my life.

We begin by judging ourselves, but once we have judged ourselves we are able to judge our brothers and sisters. This is a Christian connection. This relationship of judging one another or holding one another accountable is between the families of faith. A believer should not appoint himself or herself as a committee of one to judge any and everything wrong in the world. We do not have the right to judge everyone, and not even every believer. A wise person once said, "Advice not requested is usually not appreciated." Two believers should agree to be accountable to one another. They should sit down to discuss and agree on to what level of accountability they will hold each other. Accountability in any other way will most likely make for bad relationships and hurt feelings. Accountability is healthy and good for your Christian life, but if being accountable is not mutually agreed upon, or if one party abuses accountability, a relationship can be destroyed.

Just as a spotter can see things unseen to the driver during the race, there will be things in your life you cannot see. Other people who love you and know you can be very helpful in watching out for you. Accountability partners should be people whom we respect. They should be people who love us and do not have to earn our respect. They should have already earned the right to hold us accountable by demonstrating their love to us.

My wife, Ann, has been my most effective accountability partner in life. She loves me and has proven her love over time. She has been a faithful and devoted friend. When she says things to me that I might not like, I know she's saying them out of love and only after she has thought about them very carefully. She is often reluctant to tell me some things because she knows I may be hurt or misunderstand her words. Having earned my respect and love, I know that when she judges me she does so out of love. I appreciate the fact that she makes me a better person. She sees the things happening around me because she has a better view of my life.

When to Judge

When judging yourself, you should be judging everything all the time. When judging a brother or sister, you must build a level of trust and confidence before you can judge others.

Every day that goes by we must look openly and honestly into the secret places of our own lives. Sin in our lives is a distraction from the joy of the Lord. Sin separates us from God's best, and no amount of sin, big or small, should be allowed to remain in our lives. Everything must be exposed before the eyes of the one who sees all. "Nothing in all creation is hidden from God's sight. Everything is uncovered and laid bare before the eyes of him to whom we must give account" (Hebrews 4:13).

While we may be able to hide things from others, we can be sure that we cannot hide anything from God. Sin in our lives keeps us from seeing God clearly. Sin keeps us from being a help to our brothers and sisters in Christ. Sin is like a two-by-four stuck in our eye. Sin keeps us from seeing clearly to assist others. We have a responsibility to help others with their "blind spots," but we are not helpful when our view is obstructed.

You may think that the obstruction in your eyes is a small thing— compared to what others are doing, your sin is pretty small. I want to remind you that even a speck in your eye can be uncomfortable. A small blade of grass or a wood shaving stuck in my eye has caused some of my greatest discomfort. I tried many things to clear my eye. I rinsed with water. I used eye drops. I looked in the mirror and tried to remove the object with tweezers. Until I had someone shine a light on the area and look *for* me, everything I did was useless. Because their eye was unobstructed, they could see clearly. Once the object was removed, I felt so much better. I want to be that person for my brothers and sisters. I want to help them, because I know the discomfort associated with having a speck in my spiritual eye; however, God will not use me to help my brother until I deal with what is in my own eye.

The importance of helping our brother should create the desire in us to judge ourselves all the time. Take every opportunity the Lord provides for you to examine every detail of your life. That way, when your brother or sister is in need, you'll be ready to help.

Anyone can stray from God. Even the most devoted believers have been overtaken by sin in their lives. No one is exempt from temptation or the tempter. As we partner together in the race, we can help each other finish well. Sometimes the issue may not be sin. A believer can be overtaken by doctrinal error. "When Peter came to Antioch, I opposed him to his face, because he was clearly in the wrong. Before certain men came from James, he used to eat with Gentiles. But when they arrived, he began to draw back and separate himself from the Gentiles because he was afraid of those who belonged to the circumcision group. The other Jews join him in his hypocrisy, so that by their hypocrisy even Barnabas was led astray" (Galatians 2:11–14).

That was a doctrinal issue needing to be handled, and Paul said he held Peter accountable. There was no rivalry or hard feelings between those men, because later in the book of 1 Peter, Peter referred to Paul with kind words. Peter had been overtaken in a difficult situation. He was being two-faced about Gentiles coming to Christ. Paul said that Peter once ate with Gentiles, but when the Jewish believers put some pressure on Peter not to eat with them, he caved into the pressure. Peter could not have it both ways. If eating with Gentiles was all right, then Peter was not to change his actions just because certain people thought he was wrong. Paul thought the issue was serious enough to confront Peter. The two came to terms. They agreed. They worked out their disagreement. Paul helped Peter with a "blind spot" in his life.

Accountability says we care. When we get to heaven, we will thank the people who assisted us in this life. We will appreciate those who have loved us enough to draw attention to our "blind spots." When a spotter warns the driver of danger ahead, he does this to keep him out of trouble. An accountability partner in life can help you to avoid the danger awaiting you. You may not be able to see the danger ahead. An accountability partner is there to help you rather than to step on your freedoms. Having people in your life who care enough to watch over you is a blessing.

"Obey your leaders and submit to their authority. They keep watch over you as men who must give an account. Obey them so that their work will be a joy, not a burden, for that would be of no advantage to you" (Hebrews 13:17). You may think that what you do is no one else's business. You may think this is between you and God alone. In truth, God places people in our lives to watch over us and to make our actions their business. Our responsibility is to submit to them so they can serve with joy. We can make things easier on them by willingly submitting. That will make life better for us because they will watch over us with joy. They will not consider watching over us to be a burden when we submit to them. When watching over us is a burden, it becomes a disadvantage for us. When people watch over us with joy, it is to our advantage. They take joy in helping us because they know we appreciate what they are doing. As a pastor, I can tell you there is joy in helping people who want to be helped. People who appreciate the work of a spiritual overseer are a joy. I would encourage you to set up an appointment with your pastor and inform him of your plans to seek an accountability partner. Let him know you will appreciate him for helping you to identify any "blind spots" in your life.

How to Judge

The person who helps spot "blind spots" should be gentle and watchful, according to Galatians 6:1. Humility is the model of the Christian life. Jesus taught that, in order to be first, one must be willing to be last. If you are in an accountability role with someone, you should identify with his or her struggles. You may not struggle in the same area of temptation as he or she, but you must not give the appearance that you are better or more spiritual. Everyone has faults, and everyone struggles in certain areas of life. You cannot say your weak areas of life are any less important than others, or that theirs are less important than yours. We all must strive for the "high calling" in Christ Jesus (Philippians 3:14).

The person you select to help spot your "blind spots" should also be a person who understands that we are all sinners saved by grace. There should be forgiveness and understanding expressed by both individuals, at the same time as pursuing a life of holiness. God has called us to live holy lives. We have been set apart by Jesus Christ to be different from society. Accountability partners should help us achieve holiness without condemning or using guilt to manipulate our behavior. Guilt will defeat your life in time.

This type of accountability is developed over time, and it comes through testing. You will have to earn a person's trust. They should earn yours. The more times you are placed in situations where you are trusted the more trust you will earn. The same is true for the person you select to hold you accountable in life. That person will prove over time if he or she can be trusted with the secrets of your life. You will gain credibility with people through times of your own testing. When people see how you handle your own trials in life, they will feel freer to share their experiences with you.

The most effective way to select an accountability partner is by establishing a relationship with someone. When you build healthy relationships with people, you will not want to disappoint them. My father is the most patient man I have ever known. He loves his two sons. He always wanted what was best for us. When I was a teenager, I never wanted to disappoint my father. He was not demanding nor did he place huge expectations on my life. He is a good man. He never hurt anyone or took advantage of people. The thought of a police officer or some other civil authority having to come to my home and tell my father that his son had been taken to jail was something I didn't want to imagine. I know that I disappointed him at times, but the thought of seeing his face at a time like that motivated me to stay away from drugs and alcohol as a teenager. When you value a relationship, you will not want to disappoint that person.

Those relationships exist in local churches where believers meet together and worship the Lord. Part of the purpose of the local church is to help us hold one another accountable. When we get to heaven, we will most likely appreciate everyone who helped us in life. We will thank those who cared enough to call us when we were troubled or who took the time to come and see us when we slipped away from the Lord. Even secular organizations have learned the value of account-ability groups. In many recovery programs, people are encouraged to get into accountability groups where they can talk to someone about their struggles. They are urged not to go through life alone but to be honest when they are tempted and fall off the wagon. If those outside of Jesus Christ can find a safety net through this type of accountability, then surely we can find safety in the church. The safest place in the world ought to be in the church of Jesus Christ. People should be able to "confess their faults" one to another and know that we will not run to tell someone what we have heard.

That reminds me of the three pastors who took a retreat each year at the same cabin. They were fishing one morning and decided they would take the opportunity to confess to each other their deepest secrets and sins. The first pastor confessed that every once in a while he liked to have a drink and that from time to time he "tied one on" and got drunk. The second pastor confessed that he had been involved with another woman. He regretted this deeply, but it just happened. The third pastor was a little reluctant to share his deepest secret with the others. The other two insisted that they had told their secrets so he must also tell his. The third pastor then replied, "If you must know, I have a real problem with gossip. I can't wait to get home and tell someone what I have heard here today."

You will want to make sure that the person you ask to serve as your spotter in life can be trusted with your deepest secrets and sins. If you will be this type of person for someone, that person will most likely reciprocate. Spotters tell their drivers when they see potential danger ahead, and by listening to their spotters, the drivers have a better chance of avoiding accidents and finishing the race.

Do You Need a Drink?

The second half of this book will focus on some of the things that can cause us to be disqualified from the race. Before moving to Part Two, however, I have one more important item to be addressed in pit row. Until now, the focus has been on the automobile. The attention has been directed toward gasoline, tires, and batteries. All of those items are part of the car. But the pit crew also assists the *driver*. A few years back, the drivers were refreshed during the race differently than today. Today the drivers have the equipment to keep cold drinks in their cars. They drink through tubes attached to their helmets. But in years past, if you looked closely enough and quickly enough during a pit stop, you could see a member of the crew passing a drink to the driver. On a hot day at Texas Motor Speedway, a driver can lose a lot of fluid. A cold drink can be very refreshing.

Servicing the car and driver are both important. The car needs enough fuel to finish the race, good tires to remain stable during the race, a strong battery to last throughout the race, and a clean windshield so the driver can see the race. Assisting the driver during the race is also important. Without the driver, the car is just a machine. There have been rare occasions when a driver was not able to finish, and the team changed drivers during the race.

A cold drink on a hot day can refresh a driver and help his attitude. A person's attitude is very important to how he or she runs the race. If you are discouraged and feel like the weight of the world is on your shoulders, you are less likely to run a good race. Encouragement along the way can be a tremendous lift for the rest of the race. I hope this chapter will help lift your attitude.

"Let us hold unswervingly to the hope we profess, for He who promised is faithful. And let us consider how we may spur one another on toward love and good deeds. Let us not give up meeting together, as some are in the habit of doing, but let us encourage one another—and all the more as you see the Day approaching" (Hebrews 10:23–25).

There are three statements in these verses that begin with the words "let us"—let us hold unswervingly, let us consider, and let us not give up meeting together. God wants to inspire these things in our lives. I can almost imagine the writer of Hebrews, like a fan in the stands, yelling these words through a megaphone. These three areas are where many of us struggle and become discouraged in life. There are always circumstances that turn out differently than we planned or than how we may have expected. Some of the great men of the Bible became discouraged and needed encouragement.

> Now Ahab told Jezebel everything Elijah had done and how he had killed all the prophets with the sword. So Jezebel sent a messenger to Elijah to say, "May the gods deal with me, be it ever so severely, if by this time tomorrow I do not make your life like that of one of them." Elijah was afraid and ran for his life. When he came to Beersheba in Judah, he left his servant there, while he himself went a day's journey into the desert. He came to a broom tree, sat down under it and prayed that he might die. "I have had enough, Lord," he said. "Take my life; I am no better than my ancestors."
>
> —1 Kings 19:1–4

Earlier, Elijah stood on Mount Carmel and challenged the prophets of Baal. He came away victorious. Elijah was a great man and experienced victory on Mount Carmel. He had hardly come down from the mountain when he discovered Jezebel was out to kill him. Elijah took refuge under a juniper tree. While sitting there, Elijah became discouraged over his situation and begged God to let him die. That is a much different picture of Elijah than the one standing on Mount Carmel calling down fire from heaven. Even God's best are often discouraged.

"We do not want you to be uninformed, brothers, about the hardships we suffered in the province of Asia. We were under great pressure, far beyond our ability to endure, so that we despaired even of life. Indeed, in our hearts we felt the sentence of death. But this happened that we might not rely on ourselves but on God, who raises the dead" (2 Corinthians 1:8–9).

The great apostle Paul wrote those words. You remember him! He is the one who said, "For me to live is Christ but to die is gain." He was not afraid of anything or anyone. Paul found himself in unknown territory. He wanted the believers in Corinth to understand how difficult his life really was. He thought things were so bad that death was better than life. You may have been there before. Maybe you once had thoughts of suicide. Suicide is a major cause of death in America today. A person who is not a believer in Christ and does not have the "blessed hope" could easily find reasons to take his or her own life. Unfortunately, the suicide statistics for death among believers is far too high as well.

I wonder today, do you need a drink? Are you in need of encouragement? The verses in Hebrews exhort us to encourage others in three areas: our doubts, our deeds, and our duty.

Our Doubts

"Let us hold unswervingly to the hope we profess" (Hebrews 10:23).

Swerving can cause others to wreck. Many times we swerve in our faith. Everyone has doubts. Living by faith does not mean you will never doubt. Living by faith means we learn how to *deal* with our doubts. A man came to Jesus' apostles, in Mark, chapter 9, with a son possessed by evil spirits. The apostles attempted to exorcise the evil spirits from the boy but failed. When Jesus arrived and saw the dispute among the people, He called for the child's father. He inquired how long the child had been in that condition. After telling Jesus his child had been that way since childhood, he asked Jesus to help. Jesus said to him, "Everything is possible for him who believes" (Mark 9:23). The boy's father replied, "I do believe; help me overcome my unbelief!" (Mark 9:24).

I have felt that way many times. I believe in God, and I know Jesus Christ is the way to heaven, but I have a difficult time trusting God for the every-day decisions of life. Maybe you can relate to the man who said, "Lord, I know you parted the waters of the Red Sea, but this house payment is $1,254.69." Maybe you have expressed similar thoughts before. You know God is active, but sometimes you think He just doesn't care. Maybe He is not there!

If John the Baptist could ask Jesus if He was the Messiah, then you can be sure there will be times in your life you will doubt. Every honest person would have to admit they have doubted. So what can we do when we have doubts?

Prayer and Doubt

The Bible is filled with honest prayers where men and women talked to God openly and honestly about how they felt. The Book of Psalms contains many prayers where David poured out his feelings to God. God is already aware of our emotions and feelings before we pray. He knows what we are thinking, and He knows what we will ask for before we ask. He surely knows when we are having a bad day and are filled with doubts. The apostle Paul understood believers can be discouraged enough to doubt God. He writes, "If we are faithless, He will remain faithful, for He cannot disown Himself" (2 Timothy 2:13). There could come a time in your Christian life when you become so discouraged that you would deny Christ, but Christ will never deny you. He is our faithful witness that we belong to the Father. Even though you may choose to disown Him, He will never disown you. So pray about your doubts! Be honest with God when you pray. God can handle it. If He deserves anything from us, He deserves our honesty.

I am not suggesting a believer should take out anger and frustration on God. We owe God the utmost respect and reverence. But you are safe in telling God how you are feeling. Our privilege as sons and daughters is to share openly and honestly with our Heavenly Father. You may discover that by being honest with God when you doubt, He will help you overcome your doubts.

The Bible and Doubt

"Consequently, faith comes through hearing the message, and the message is heard through the word of Christ" (Romans 10:17). God uses the stories and principles taught in the Bible to strengthen our faith. Some have the idea that trials strengthen faith, but trials are God's way of revealing our faith. Trials are like an exam where God is revealing to us the kind of faith we possess. How many times have you gone through an experience and thought, "I didn't handle that very well. I sure could have done things differently, and if given the chance I *will* do things differently." You can be sure that God will give you the opportunity.

Dr. John Pretlove was one of my professors in college. Every time Dr. Pretlove would give an exam to the class he would say, "This is your opportunity to do good." Most of the students did not agree. We thought tests were opportunities to fail. But Dr. Pretlove was correct. If we had studied the assignments and done our homework, the grade on the exam would be good. The exam gave us the opportunity to prove that we had learned the material.

God gives us opportunities in life to reveal our faith. He allows situations to develop in life where we can demonstrate our faith. If we fail to demonstrate faith in a certain situation, we can be sure that God will give us another opportunity.

God believes in "make-up exams." He gives us every opportunity to do well. When things happen in life to reveal our faith, they direct us to the Word of God. When we read the stories of how Daniel survived the night in the lions' den or how young David defeated a nine-foot, nine-inch-tall Philistine giant, we are inspired and our faith is strengthened. The stories were written for us, according to Paul in 1 Corinthians 10:6. God included them in the Bible in order to show us that little is much when God is in it. Faith is what overcomes doubt, and if you ever plan to strengthen your faith, you must read the Word of God.

Sharing and Doubt

Relationships with mature believers are important. Those who have "been there, done that" prove to be a valuable asset in life. They can help you when you doubt and offer encouragement through personal experiences. Every believer should aspire to be an encourager. People have problems, and in life they sometimes just need someone to listen. A man was driving down the road one day and came to a bridge. He noticed another man standing on the edge of the bridge about to jump. The driver asked the man if he could sit down with him for a minute before he took his life and talk with him about what was wrong. The man agreed, and they both sat down on the edge of the bridge. About thirty minutes later, they both jumped off the bridge. Obviously, that was not a very helpful man.

Mature believers can be very supportive for those struggling with doubts. God allows us to go through situations so we can assist others. Perhaps God has someone in your life who can listen to you when you are discouraged. If you have not built a relationship with a mature believer who will listen, you should pray that God will bring this person into your life. Everyone needs someone with whom he or she can share openly and honestly the happenings in life. In fact, all believers ought to have relationships with other believers who are more mature and less mature than themselves. That way you will have people helping you in life, and you will be helping others in life. The Christian life is all about others. We are taught in the Bible to love one another, pray for one another, and admonish one another. You will have doubts, and when you do, you should talk to someone who understands, because they have been where you are.

Our Deeds

"And let us consider how we may spur one another on toward love and good deeds" (Hebrews 10:24).

In the 1960s, there was a show on television called "Stoney Burke." The show starred Jack Lord, who traveled the circuit riding in rodeos. The show did not last very long, but that was not my fault. I can tell you I was the show's biggest fan. I rarely watched television as a child, because watching television interfered with my time playing sports. When "Stoney" came on television, though, I was in front of the TV set. I dreamed of being Stoney Burke and riding horses in the rodeo. I had the blue jean jacket and black hat like he wore. I remember one year specifically receiving spurs for Christmas. I strapped the spurs to my boots, and I wore those spurs everywhere. You could hear me coming for blocks because of the clanging of those spurs. I liked to hear them clang. So I made sure I rubbed the heel of my boots together so those spurs would clang. The day finally came when I got to ride a horse. The horse did not mind the spurs as long as they just made noise. But when I kicked those spurs into the horse's side, he was not a happy camper. Let's just say that on that particular day I learned I was no Stoney Burke. When I put those spurs into the side of that horse, I discovered the horse had a gear I had never seen before.

As believers, we have the opportunity to help other believers discover they can do better than they thought possible. We can inspire other believers to love the way God loves. We have the wonderful privilege of helping other believers do good deeds for Jesus Christ. Perhaps the most effective way to spur others is through our own example. People will follow a good example. By being a good example to others, we can inspire them to do the same. Jesus taught that we are to be salt and light to the world. That means we should make the world a better place to live and help point others in the right direction. The world is not as impressed by our words as they are by our works. Telling people to do as we say is not enough. We must be able to say to them, "Do as we do."

"In everything set them an example by doing what is good. In your teaching show integrity, seriousness and soundness of speech that cannot be condemned, so that those who oppose you may be ashamed because they have nothing bad to say about us" (Titus 2:7–8). In this Scripture, Paul exhorts Titus to be a good example. The Greek word for example is "tupon." The idea of this word is to be a pattern. In other words, Paul is exhorting Titus to show the people a pattern of what doing good should look like. Every believer should be a pattern for doing what is good. Good deeds inspire others to do better. When a Christian sets an example by doing good deeds, other believers are inspired. When they witness the joy that comes by doing good deeds, they are likely to want the same joy. Jesus taught that true joy comes by serving and not by being served. Your random acts of kindness will be an inspiration to others.

Another way we can inspire others to do good deeds is through words of encouragement. "Teach slaves to be subject to their masters in everything, to try to please them, not to talk back to them, and not to steal from them, but to show that they can be fully trusted, so that in every way they will make the teaching about God our Savior attractive" (Titus 2:9). An encouraging word will help inspire others. The night before Jesus was crucified, He ate the Passover Meal with His disciples. He told the disciples that one of them would betray Him. They all begin to wonder which one would betray Jesus, and even searched their own consciences asking, "Is it I?" Peter was a little insulted by the insinuation. He went so far as to tell Christ, that he would die for Christ, that he would never deny Christ. Then Jesus spoke to Peter these words: "Simon, Simon, Satan has asked to sift you as wheat. But I have prayed for you, Simon, that your faith may not fail. And when you have turned back, strengthen your brothers" (Luke 22:31–32).

Those words may not have meant as much to Peter then as they did later on, but they are very powerful. Not only was Jesus praying for Peter, but also Jesus believed in Peter. Jesus said, "When you have turned back . . . ," which implies that Jesus knew Peter *would* turn back. He knew Peter would deny Him three times, but He also knew Peter would turn back. Nothing could be more encouraging than to know the Savior believes in you. When other people believe in you, you can do almost anything. As believers, we need to encourage other believers with our words. We ought to be standing behind people, encouraging them to do good deeds. Let people know you believe in them. Remind them that they have the Holy Spirit living in them to assist them in anything God asks them to do. Spurs in a horse's side will remind the horse that he or she has a gear he or she may not have used in a long time.

Experience is another excellent way to inspire good deeds from others. Once you have tasted how good helping others feels, you will want more. You will not be satisfied to sit idly by and watch others serve. Serving others is contagious. There is a spiritual high associated with helping others and watching God work in a person's life. There are many in your neighborhood and at your place of employment who need to be encouraged. They are discouraged and need someone to set an example or to speak inspiring words that motivate them to do good deeds. What are you waiting for?

Our Duty

"Let us not give up meeting together, as some are in the habit of doing, but let us encourage one another—and all the more as you see the Day approaching" (Hebrews 10:25).

Attending church should not be optional for the believer. Christ established His church. By not attending church, a believer is discrediting what Christ died to build. There are many excuses people give for why they are not faithfully attending church: "There are too many hypocrites in the church!" "All they want is my money!" "I can worship at home!" These excuses will be pretty lame when we stand before the Judgment Seat of Christ. The church is the assembly of God's redeemed on earth. Until the day God gathers all the redeemed of all the ages into one place, the local church is the place Christ established for believers to meet. If Christ could die for the church, we certainly should faithfully attend His church.

The local church is a great place to inspire good deeds in others. Even though there are hypocrites in the church, you can be sure there are hypocrites *everywhere*. Some churches may abuse the subject of giving. This does not lessen the idea that God wants each believer to faithfully tithe on their income. We can worship at home, but Hebrews 10:25 directly addresses the importance of corporate worship in the church. We should worship at home *and* in local churches.

Working together in local churches is what Christ had in mind when He established the church. What a concept! What an opportunity! In the local church, we have the opportunity to exercise our spiritual gifts and natural talents for the Lord. Because of the local church, there are multitudes of opportunities for believers to serve God. I am a pastor, and God gives me the privilege each week of exercising my gift of teaching in the local church where I serve. I am by no means the best preacher in the world. If the church were to assemble in only one place, I would most likely be the last guy they asked to speak to the crowd. But in the local church where I serve, I get to preach each week. The same thing is true for every member. Each believer has the opportunity to use his or her gifts and talents for the Lord in a local church. Everyone can and should be using their gifts and talents. When we do, the gospel spreads more rapidly.

The early believers had to leave Jerusalem because of persecution. The apostles remained in Jerusalem, but the people scattered. As they scattered from city to city, they went everywhere, using their gifts and preaching the gospel. That is God's will today. God's will is for believers to participate in local churches and use their gifts, talents, and tithes to help spread the gospel. From time to time, there will be some in the church who will have doubts. They will need to be encouraged. You may have doubts. Maybe you will get discouraged and be defeated by something that happens in your life. I am sure you would appreciate another believer coming alongside of you and encouraging you.

Do you need a drink today? Be a part of the team, encouraging others around you. You will probably discover that they are also God's team, helping to encourage you in the race.

PART II
PITFALLS

Stay Fit

J eff Gordon spent Wednesday night, December 1, 2004, in the hospital because of flu-like symptoms. This kept him from racing in a head-to-head matchup with Formula One ace Michael Schumacher Saturday in Paris. Gordon and Hendrick Motorsports teammate Jimmie Johnson were scheduled to represent the USA in the Race of Champions Nations Cup, an international all-star event. "He's definitely under the weather," Johnson said. "And being as dehydrated as he is with the flu symptoms, being on an airplane for eight hours is probably not a good move."

Every racecar driver's goal is to celebrate in Victory Lane. They enter the race to win. When they win, they celebrate in Victory Lane. Vince Lombardi once said, "If it does not matter who wins or loses, then why keep score?" Lombardi was one of the greatest football coaches in history. The racecar driver might say, "If it doesn't matter who wins or loses, why celebrate in Victory Lane?" The winner *does* matter to teams and their fans. Teams require sponsors and owners to back them financially. Those investors want their money to support winners. Teams earn points each week. At the end of the year, the team with the most points is crowned the Cup-champion. While there are more ways to earn points than winning a race on Sunday, winning is the goal of each team and driver. Teams work together for approximately three hours each Sunday to be the team in Victory Lane.

There are challenges each week that prohibit some from finishing the race. Forty-three cars begin the race, but not all will finish. I have spent the first half of this book writing about the activities pit crews perform to help the driver finish the race. I have compared those activities to how God helps us in the Christian race. God provides the fuel for the race. He has given us the Bible, the Word of God. He changes our tires through worship so we can have proper balance. He allows us to fellowship with other believers so we can be energized for the race. He allows us to talk to Him through prayer so we can know exactly what we need for the race. He provides accountability partners so they can help identify the "blind spots" in our lives. He refreshes us with the local church so we can stay encouraged throughout the race.

In the second half of this book I want to address some of the things that can disqualify a car and driver from the race. Just as there are things that happen in a road race to disqualify drivers, there are things that happen in life that can disqualify you and me from the race that God has marked out for us. Satan puts things in our path to disqualify us from the race. Not every driver will end up in "Victory Lane." Forty-three cars start the race, but only one will win. In the Christian race, however, *every* contestant can win. In a NASCAR race, drivers compete for up to three hours, under extreme conditions. Drivers must maintain good physical condition in order to compete each week. In the Christian race, we must remain in top spiritual condition in order to finish the race well. The first obstacle in the race of life is you.

"'Everything is permissible for me,' but not everything is beneficial. 'Everything is permissible for me,' but I will not be mastered by anything" (1 Corinthians 6:12).

"Do you not know that your body is a temple of the Holy Spirit, who is in you, whom you have received from God? You are not your own; you were bought at a price. Therefore honor God with your body" (1 Corinthians 6:19–20).

There are many obstacles you will face in life. The biggest obstacle is you. As born-again believers, we belong to Jesus Christ. He has moved into our lives. Our bodies have become His home. He lives in us. However, the old sin nature still remains. Satan uses the weak areas of our sin nature and plants things in the way to appeal to our old sin nature. We must guard ourselves against the strongholds Satan places in our path. The word "stronghold" means "fortress." The Bible says, "The weapons we fight with are not the weapons of the world. On the contrary, they have divine power to demolish strongholds" (2 Corinthians 10:4).

Satan will take weak areas of your life and build fortresses around them. Tearing down those fortresses once he has built them is not easy.

There is a lot of truth in the old saying: "If you give Satan an inch, he will take a foot." We must be cautious about giving Satan any opportunity to get a stronghold in our lives. Taking down strongholds can be more difficult than allowing Satan to build a stronghold in your life.

Ann and I have three children. As each of our children was in his or her senior year of high school, I took a trip with him or her individually. We took family vacations each year, but this was different. This was a trip for each child to celebrate his or her individual accomplishments. This was my way of commending them for being great children. This was our father and child time. Each child and each trip holds special memories for them and me. Our youngest daughter, Olivia, asked to go to Maui for her senior trip. I say she *asked*, but when a blonde-haired, blue-eyed baby daughter bats her pretty eyes at Daddy, she doesn't really ask, she tells you what you are going to do. She told me we were going to Maui, and that is where we went.

On the final evening in Maui, we attended a Luau. The inclement weather required the Luau to be moved inside, but we didn't mind. As we walked into the banquet room, they snapped our picture together and offered us drinks. There were alcoholic and non-alcoholic drinks. Jokingly, I asked my daughter if she wanted an alcoholic drink, to which she replied "no." We were there to celebrate her graduation from high school and thousands of miles from anyone who knew us, especially her mother. She still said no! I was so proud. So I asked her later that evening why she'd said no. My daughter, the little princess I had watched grow to be a young woman said, "Because I do not want to like it!"

What a wise girl. Her mother must have done a great job. To my knowledge, I never taught her that. Later, Ann confessed that she'd never taught her that either. Olivia understood that it is better to never start than to start and try to quit. Never allowing something to become a stronghold in your life is better than trying to take something back later. Many have failed to stand strong against temptation. They have allowed Satan to get a stronghold in their lives. Our bodies do not belong to Satan or even to ourselves any more.

Our bodies are the temple of the Holy Spirit, according to 1 Corinthians 6:19. The word translated as "temple" is from the Greek word "naos." That was the word used for the "Holy of Holies" when the Old Testament Hebrew Bible was translated into Greek. The "Holy of Holies" was the room beyond the veil in the Holy Place where the Ark of the Covenant rested. Above the Ark of the Covenant were two Cherubim. The two Cherubim faced each other, and between them was the glory of God. God's presence was beyond the veil inside the Holy of Holies. He met with the High Priest inside the Holy of Holies each year on the Day of Atonement.

When Jesus died on the cross, there followed certain phenomena. The Scriptures record an earthquake followed by thundering and lightening. Graves were opened, and the veil of the temple was torn from top to bottom. The veil that separated the Holy Place from the Holy of Holies was approximately four inches thick of layered material. Only a miracle and an act of God could tear that veil in half. But that is what happened the day Jesus died on the cross. The Heavenly Father was making a powerful statement. The way to God was no longer through animal sacrifices. Access to the Father was now through His Son Jesus Christ. God no longer resides beyond a veil. God dwells in the hearts of His people. Our bodies belong to the Holy Spirit. They are the living quarters of the Holy Spirit and should be used in His service.

I would not want you to be disqualified in the race because you allowed Satan to build a stronghold in your life. Satan is always prowling and looking for believers he can tempt and lead astray. As the Bible states, "Be self controlled and alert. Your enemy the devil prowls around like a roaring lion looking for someone to devour" (1 Peter 5:8).

Satan awaits the opportunity to exploit your weak areas and build a fortress around what he has conquered. But you can stay fit for the race. In order to stay fit in the race of life, I want to encourage you to consider your choices, consider your challenges, and consider your character.

Consider your Choices

"Everything is permissible but not everything is beneficial" (1 Corinthians 6:12). The apostle Paul understood he was free to choose. Being saved and kept by grace means we are no longer under the law of the Old Testament. Paul understood grace better than anyone. He fought for our right to choose to live by grace. Grace is not a license to sin. As born-again believers, we are motivated by our love for God, not the law. There is a law written in our hearts more binding than the law written on the tablets of stone. We do not need a list of rules in order to live for God. The greatest law is to love God with your whole heart. Jesus defined this as the most important law. "Jesus replied: 'Love the Lord your God with all your heart and with all your soul and with all your mind. This is the first and greatest commandment'" (Matthew 22:37–38).

If we love God with all our hearts, we are not likely to make choices that will displease Him. Everyone is affected by his or her choices, and life is filled with choices. The Bible does not address every choice you make with a black or white answer. Life would be much easier if it did. Life would be wonderful if every choice were addressed with a clear commandment from Scripture. But that's not the way things happen. The Bible provides principles to guide your choices. One such principle is the one that says, "We belong to God" (1 Corinthians 6:19–20).

Because we belong to God, we must not allow things to enter our lives that will harm our walk with God. Even though we may be free, this does not mean everything we do is beneficial for us. Anything that takes over your life or controls you has the potential of taking God's place in your life as first. Most believers love God. The struggle for many believers is to love God the most. To love God with all our hearts, souls, and minds is to put God above any and everything else in our lives. When we allow things to control our lives, we become the slave of that object. God has never wanted His people to be slaves to anyone or anything. He redeemed Israel from Egypt because He chose them to be free people belonging to Him. He redeemed us so we could be free to serve Him as His own people.

> For the grace of God that brings salvation has appeared to all men. It teaches us to say "No!" to ungodliness and worldly passions, and to live self-controlled, upright and godly lives in this present age, while we wait for the blessed hope—the glorious appearing of our great God and Savior, Jesus Christ, who gave himself for us to redeem us from all wickedness

and to purify for himself a people that are his very own, eager to do what is good.

—Titus 2:11–14

You can be sure that Satan will tempt you in the areas where you are the most vulnerable. He sets traps for us in life where he has witnessed our weaknesses. He is not omnipresent. He cannot be in more than one place at one time. He has demons that act as scouts for him and watch our weak areas so he can tempt us. He uses those weak areas to build strongholds in our lives. The Holy Spirit is not controlling a believer who is controlled by an addiction. Evaluate the things you allow in your life. The Holy Spirit should not have to share space in your life. If your body is the temple of the Holy Spirit, you belong to God, and that principle should guide the choices you make.

Besides taking control of our lives and becoming our master, the choices we make also affect our witness. As born-again believers, our responsibility is to show Christ to others. You and I are the only Bible some people read. We are Christ's witnesses, and our responsibility is to reflect Christ in a positive manner. The world has a right to hold believers to a higher standard because Christ lived by a higher standard. The word "Christian" means "Christ-like." The word was used initially in the city of Antioch, because the early believers reminded the people of what they had heard about Jesus Christ. Being a Christian means we have chosen to follow Jesus Christ. We have given our lives to Him for His Kingdom, and we have made the choice to serve Him. The Christian life involves many choices. Our lives must not cause others to stumble or to question the reality of God. The choices we make speak volumes to the world. The world watches us and pays close attention to where we go and what we do. You can spend years establishing credibility with someone who is not a believer and destroy your credibility in minutes because of a poor choice.

Consider your Challenges

"The body is meant for the Lord and the Lord for the body" (1 Corinthians 6:13). Our bodies become an instrument for God to use. In the same way the pit crew would use a jack or a tire tool, God uses us to do his work. Our goal should be to make our bodies a servant, not a master. Paul compared being filled with the Spirit to be being drunk with wine in Ephesians 5:18. The reason it is wrong to be drunk with wine is because the wine takes over your life. When a person is drunk, he or she is under the control of alcohol. The Holy Spirit is to control our lives. We should be under the controlling influence of the Holy Spirit and nothing else. Addiction of any kind will put you under the control of your body rather than the Spirit.

"No, I beat my body and make it my slave so that after I have preached to others, I myself will not be disqualified for the prize" (1 Corinthians 9:27). The apostle Paul was a fierce competitor. He was motivated to win. He realized his greatest competition was with himself. His own body could disqualify him. He worked to keep his body the slave rather than allowing his body to become his master. Our bodies do not belong to us once Christ moves in. Our bodies become His instrument of service and must be yielded to Him rather than personal pleasure. Paul knew he was no longer under the law of the Old Testament. He knew he was free to eat and drink anything he wanted. By denying his body certain pleasures, he was in control.

We all have challenges. What is a weakness in one person may be another person's strength. You can be sure that Satan will exploit each of our weaknesses. He will set traps where we are the weakest, not where we're strong. You may need to take ownership of a weak area. You may need to notify an accountability partner so you can have victory over your weakness. Admitting your weakness is not an act of weakness. The first step to victory is admitting there is a problem. Treat your body as your instrument of service to God and the home of the Holy Spirit. Whatever you do, you involve the Holy Spirit because He is our companion in life. He never leaves us. He is always with us, and we should consider this when we face our challenges.

When I was about twenty years old, the owner of the company where I was employed invited me to take a ride in his new Jaguar. The car was a beauty, and sitting in the passenger seat did not quite do enough for me. I was "all smiles" when he asked, "Would you like to drive it?" I could not wait to get behind the wheel of that car. I had never driven anything like that before. I could see myself flying down the road, passing everyone in sight and having some real fun. So he handed me the keys, and I got behind the wheel. I was about to take off when the front passenger door opened and my employer took a seat beside me. His presence changed everything! I could not drive the way I wanted to drive because he was with me. He spoiled my fun, although he may have saved my life.

The difference was having him in the car. His presence with me made me "highway Bob," like you see on the drivers' training videos. I was careful. I checked to see that my speed was correct. I looked in the mirrors before changing lanes. I took slow turns, and I never burned the tires one time. That taught me a lesson about how we should treat our bodies. We need to understand that God is with us all the time. He is there when we give in to our weakness, and like it or not, we involve the Holy Spirit in our sinful activity.

> Food for the stomach and the stomach for food—but God will destroy them both. The body is not meant for sexual immorality, but for the Lord, and the Lord for the body. By his power God raised the Lord from the dead, and he will raise us also. Do you not know that your bodies are members of Christ himself? Shall I then take the members of Christ and unite them with a prostitute? Never! Do you not know that he who unites himself with a prostitute is one with her in body? For it is said, "The two will become one flesh." But he who unites himself with the Lord is one with Him in spirit. Flee from sexual immorality. All other sins a man commits are outside his body, but he who sins sexually sins against his own body.
>
> —1 Corinthians 6:13–18

Consider your Character

Your body is a member of Christ and part of the Lord's own body. "So in Christ we who are many form one body, and each member belongs to all the others" (Romans 12:5).

Sin that involves our bodies involves our Lord. When Ann and I first moved to Forney, Texas, to accept the pastorate of the Forney Baptist Church, the church was very small. In fact, there were only ten other people in the service when I came to candidate. I will never forget how we both felt when we turned into the church parking lot that Sunday. We didn't know anything about the church. All we knew about churches was what we had experienced in the one where we had grown up and the few where I had preached the first year I was in the ministry. The differences between men and women, and particularly between a pastor and his wife, were evident in what both of us were thinking as we turned into the parking lot. I was thinking, "I wonder how many people attend this church?" Ann was thinking, "I wonder if we have to live in that house behind the church?"

Like most pastors, I went to work trying to reach the people in the community. I tried to identify something about this church that connected the people, outside of their relationship to Jesus Christ. There were only four couples besides us. I began to notice that they all seemed to like wrestling. In 1978, wrestling was a lot different than it is today, and the Sportatorium in Dallas was where it all happened. That was the place of Fritz Von Erich, Spoiler I, and Spoiler II. You could see Andre the Giant and villains like Gary Hart. So I decided one Saturday night that I would go with a man from the church and, like a good pastor's wife, Ann should go with me. You would have to go yourself to have any idea what we witnessed that night.

I remember looking around at all the people and watching as they cheered and booed for their favorite wrestlers. I looked over at my sweet, innocent wife and noticed that she was not having a very good time. I made some kind of comment to which she replied, "Would you bring God in here?" I said, "I think I just did!" As a believer, there is no place we go where God does not go with us. We cannot check the Holy Spirit at the door and ask Him to wait for us outside. He is our companion for life and His home is our body.

Are you causing the Holy Spirit to participate in activities unbecoming of a Holy God? The Christian life is not all about you and your freedoms to do what you want to do. The Christian life is about reflecting the character of the one who lives in us. The best way to overcome strongholds in your life is to realize your body is an instrument of service for the Lord. Every time you allow Satan to build a fortress around a weak area of your life, you are weakened. To take back what you have given will be more difficult than not giving away something in the first place, but it is not impossible. You can reclaim the ground God has won for you at Calvary. You do not have to remain weak or continue being blackmailed by Satan. He wants you to think you can never change. By God's grace, and with God's help, you can change. Our weapons have divine power to demolish strongholds. The Bible, the Holy Spirit, worship, fellowship with other believers, prayer, and accountability are divine weapons. They will help you live the life God has called you to live.

There are many obstacles you will face in life, but none more worthy than yourself. Pogo, in the legendary cartoon strip once said, "We have met the enemy and he is us!" You can be your own worst enemy to finishing the race well, or you can be your best supporter. You do not want to be disqualified because you allowed some stronghold to master your life. The power of the Holy Spirit in you can and will enable you to defeat your sin nature and rise above your weakness. The apostle Paul did not say he could do *some things* with Christ's help. He said he could do *all* things with Christ's help (Philippians 4:13). With the companionship of the Holy Spirit who lives in us, we can master our bodies rather than allowing our bodies to master us.

As we take control of our bodies and use them in obedient service to Jesus Christ, we become fit for the race. A fit driver will last throughout the entire race and give his team the best chance to win. Changing drivers at any point in the race can cost precious time and all but assure someone else will celebrate in Victory Lane. If you expect to celebrate in Victory Lane, you must remain fit throughout the race.

Practice Makes Perfect!

Greg Biffle intended to move from the minors to the majors like most people, but he enjoyed winning the 2002 Busch championship so much that he couldn't give the series up. He believes that prosperity on one circuit leads to success on the other, especially when both races are held in the same place.

"Practice makes perfect," Biffle said. "I get two hours of practice on a track before I get in the car for the Cuprace. It keeps me acclimated all the time."

NASCAR teams and drivers spend hours in practice. Pit crews practice their techniques in order to eliminate precious seconds in the pits. Drivers practice their maneuvers to see how the car will handle on the track. Every athlete, musician, and individual with a specialized skill understands the importance of practice. Practice makes perfect, and while perfection is difficult to execute every time, perfection is what each team strives for on every race day. The key to practice is discipline.

Professional golfers spend hours a day hitting golf balls and working on their short game. Football, baseball, and basketball players perfect their skills through hours of practice. Musicians sacrifice much time in order to play their instruments well. When I was younger, I wanted to play the guitar. I did not want to *learn* to play the guitar. I just wanted to *play*—and there is an enormous difference. To learn to play the guitar I had to spend hours each day practicing. I thought I could just buy a guitar and begin to play, but I was mistaken. Each week when I would show up for my thirty minute lesson, Mr. Tyler would ask me if I had practiced one hour each day as he requested. I do not know why he asked me that question. In just a few minutes of playing the guitar for him, it became obvious I had not spent much time practicing. Had he asked me if I had spent time practicing my jump shot or throwing a curveball, I could have said yes, but the fact is that practicing the guitar interfered with my real love of sports. The reason I can only play "Oh Susanna" and a little "Boggy-woogie" on the guitar today is that I was not disciplined enough to practice.

Our oldest daughter, Tamara, on the other hand, is an excellent pianist. Her passion for music led her to practice for hours. I enjoy hearing her play the piano today more than anyone. Tamara's husband and my son-in-law, Jim, is also a fine musician. He plays the guitar the way I dreamed of playing in my childhood. Tamara and Jim perfected their skills through practice.

The same discipline required to perfect earthly skills is also necessary in the Christian race. Just as professional racecar drivers train in order to stay in good physical condition, you and I need to practice certain disciplines in our lives in order to run the race. Practicing may not be as enjoyable as the race, but practice is necessary. Spiritual disciplines in your life will help you to run a better race. They will prepare you for the road ahead and help you to avoid the debris Satan places in the road. When you practice, you learn how to handle certain situations before they actually happen. You will have practiced that move or handled that situation before. Very few things are as satisfying as winning the big race. Victory on the day of the race is the result of hours of preparation through practice, and practicing is the result of discipline.

The Reason for Discipline

You have probably discovered the battle inside for control. As a born-again believer, the Spirit of God lives in you. However, the old nature is still with us, and the old nature does not give up control easily. The old nature wants to control our actions. The Christian life is a battle, and your body is the battlefield. Many believers have not discovered the victory available through submission to the Holy Spirit.

> So I find this law at work: When I want to do good, evil is right there with me. For in my inner being I delight in God's law; but I see another law at work in the members of my body, waging war against the law of my mind and making

me prisoner of the law of sin at work within my members. What a wretched man I am! Who will rescue me from this body of death? Thanks be to God—through Jesus Christ our Lord!

—Romans 7:21–25

Our bodies are our most difficult challenge to living the Christian life. They are our most important instruments of service, and they pose the most difficulty. You may think you have defeated your old sin nature, and out of the blue it makes a surprise attack. This led Paul to conclude that there is a law at work against his body. The old nature wages war against the new nature and can make you a prisoner. You do not have to be a prisoner to the law of sin. Paul said Christ has given us victory over the old nature.

Living with the old nature can be like being chained to a dead person. When Paul asked the question, "Who will rescue me from this body of death?" he was using an analogy from the first century. Often the Romans would chain prisoners together. In some cases, when there was just one prisoner, a soldier would chain himself to the prisoner. When there were multiple prisoners, they would chain them to one another. In some cases, a prisoner would die in prison, leaving the other prisoner chained to a dead body. Besides the discomfort associated with being chained to a corpse, you can imagine how restrictive dragging a dead body around all the time would be. Living with the old nature can be like dragging around dead weight. Sin will keep you from being the person God intended you to be. Sin can keep you from being the person you would like to be. You probably do want a better life. You would like to live in victory over sinful habits. You would like to do the things you really enjoy doing for Christ, but you may feel like you are dragging around this dead person.

> You, however, are controlled not by the sinful nature but by the Spirit, if the Spirit of God lives in you. And if anyone does not have the Spirit of Christ, he does not belong to Christ. But if Christ is in you, your body is dead because of sin, yet your spirit is alive because of righteousness. And if

> the Spirit of him who raised Jesus from the dead is living in
> you, he who raised Christ from the dead will also give life to
> your mortal bodies through his Spirit, who lives in you.
> —Romans 8:9–11

Thank God for Romans, chapter 8! Romans, chapter 7 is about the law, and Romans 8 is about the Spirit. The law condemns and judges, but the Spirit sets free. If you ever plan to overcome the old nature, you must surrender to the divine nature God sent to live in you when you accepted Christ as your Savior. We do not have the right to live by the sinful nature, because we are under the management of the Spirit of Christ. He is our master! We belong to Him!

Charles Swindoll once told a story about a woman who lived on a large plantation. After many years of marriage, her husband died. She could not bear the thought of burying her husband in the ground, so she spent the money to have him preserved in a glass room inside her home. She placed him in his favorite chair over by the fireplace, where she could sit and talk with him for hours. Some time later, she took a trip. On this trip, she met a man and fell in love. They were married. The day came for them to return to her plantation. When they walked into the house, there sat her first husband. The man was rather shocked and inquired, "Who is that guy?" She informed him that he was her first husband and of how she loved him too much to bury him in the ground. Her new husband said, "Woman, he has to go! You do not belong to him any more. You belong to me!"

> What shall we say, then? Shall we go on sinning so that grace
> may increase? By no means! We died to sin; how can we live
> in it any longer? Or don't you know that all of us who were
> baptized into Christ Jesus were baptized into His death? We
> were therefore buried with Him through baptism into death
> in order that, just as Christ was raised from the dead through
> the glory of the Father, we too may live a new life.
> —Romans 6:1–4

Once you decide to make Christ the Lord of your life, your life becomes His. His Spirit moves in to live and to control every thought and every decision we make. You and I must make the choice to allow Christ to rule in our lives and not yield to the old nature. We are under a new manager. His name is Jesus Christ. We do not have the freedom to sin. We have the freedom and power to overcome sin's control. Discipline is required on our part to surrender to Christ's control and consider ourselves dead to sin.

> In the same way, count yourselves dead to sin but alive to God in Christ Jesus. Therefore do not let sin reign in your mortal body so that you obey its evil desires. Do not offer the parts of your body to sin, as instruments of wickedness, but rather offer yourselves to God, as those who have been bought from death to life; and offer the parts of your body to him as instruments of righteousness. For sin shall not be your master, because you are not under law, but under grace.
>
> —Romans 6:11–14

To consider yourself to be dead to sin is to recognize that sin no longer has a stronghold on your life. You died to sin, according to verse two. That is a great analogy, because everyone understands the finality of death. We understand that when someone dies they are not coming back in this lifetime. You will most likely have to keep reminding your old sin nature that he or she is dead. The old nature wants to live, but if Christ is living in you, the old nature must die. You must make the choice to die daily. You can say, "I am dead to sin," when you accept Christ as your Savior in hopes this will be enough, but you will soon discover you require daily discipline to count yourself dead to sin but alive to God in Jesus Christ.

One time I was on a board of trustees of a state missions organization. I served with several other men. We had the responsibility to discuss many issues about the missions and missionaries in Texas. On one particular day, we were discussing a certain missionary. We were not comfortable discussing these other men of God, but this was necessary. When issues came up about certain men, we had a responsibility to make sure that the issues were discussed and the missionary was fit for the ministry. As we discussed one particular missionary, something was discussed about a certain incident which had occurred in his past. I will never forget what one of the trustees said regarding that issue: "I think he (the missionary) is dead to that!"

I do not believe I ever heard that statement before. I was so impressed because I had not thought like this before. I understood that when Christ comes to live in your life there ought to be changes, but I never thought about it in terms of being dead to something. Considering yourself dead coincides with what Paul writes in Romans 6:11. We must consider ourselves dead to certain behaviors, habits, thoughts, and freedoms when we give our lives to become Christ's home.

There is more than just considering ourselves to be dead to sin. Paul writes in verse thirteen that we are to offer the parts of our bodies as instruments of righteousness. The same parts we once used to serve sin should now be used in service to God. The apostle Paul was zealous about everything. Before he was converted to Christ, he persecuted the church of Jesus Christ. He persecuted the church with zeal. No one was more serious about destroying the church than Saul of Tarsus (his name before he was converted). Saul breathed out threatening words against the church. He was determined to destroy the church. When he met Christ, Paul began to serve Christ with the same zeal and determination. The parts of his body once used to destroy the church were now being used to help build the church.

If we would use the energy and effort we once used to serve sin to serve God, incredible things would get done. Perhaps we could turn the world upside-down for Christ like the early church. We spend enormous amounts of time, money, and energy in pursuit of our recreational hobbies and pleasures. As born-again believers, we should now use our resources and energies to build the Kingdom of God.

The Requirements for Discipline

There are three areas of our lives requiring discipline to run an effective race. These three areas correspond to the three parts of man—spirit, soul, and body. "May God himself, the God of peace, sanctify you through and through. May your whole spirit, soul and body be kept blameless at the coming of our Lord Jesus Christ" (1 Thessalonians 5:23).

The apostle Paul could have arranged these three things in different orders. He could have written body, soul, and spirit. He could have written body, spirit, and soul. He could have written soul, spirit, and body, or soul, body, and spirit. But he wrote, "spirit, soul and body." This is the formula for successful Christian living. Any other formula will not work. You must let the spirit control the mind, and together the mind and spirit control the body, if you expect to live a successful Christian life.

Let me explain: The Spirit is the divine nature living in each believer. Even though the Spirit does not need our help, we can unleash His power through submission and obedience. The most effective way to unleash the Spirit is to obey by saying "yes." When a person accepts Christ as his or her personal Savior, that person receives all of the Spirit. God cannot be divided in portions. If He lives in a person, He moves in entirely. When the Spirit of Christ comes to live in us, He brings all of Himself. The question is "does the Spirit have all of us?" He will gain more control over your life when you yield your entire self to Him. He gives all of Himself to us. We must give all of ourselves to Him. To give God all of us means that He must be first. Every thought and every idea must be surrendered to the Spirit. "We demolish arguments and every pretension that sets itself up against the knowledge of God, and we take captive every thought to make it obedient to Christ" (2 Corinthians 10:5).

The soul refers to the mind. The Greek word for soul is "psuche." Psychology is the study of the mind. There are many things a person can change by his or her will. The mind tells a person that certain things are wrong and should be avoided. But the mind alone is not enough to help us live victorious lives. That is why Paul wrote the formula as spirit before soul. The mind does not have power over the body alone. There are people who know that certain things are wrong, but they cannot help themselves. Sometimes they even blame Satan. Even though they know a certain action is wrong, they do it anyway.

We can discipline our minds by renewing our minds. "Do not conform any longer to the pattern of this world, but be transformed by the renewing of your mind. Then you will be able to test and approve what God's will is—his good, pleasing and perfect will" (Romans 12:2). To renew your mind means to change the way you think. We must learn to think the way God thinks. God thinks about things differently. Our responsibility is to learn to think the way God thinks. You discover how God thinks by reading the Word of God. Every Christian counselor understands the importance of helping people to think the way that God thinks. The best counsel you can receive in life will come from God's Word. God's Word reveals how God thinks. Once you discover how God thinks, you must surrender to God. Knowing to surrender and actually surrendering can be two different things. As you submit to the power of the Spirit in your life, you can surrender your thoughts to His thoughts and learn to think the way that God thinks. Mind over body will not be enough, but the Spirit controlling the mind, and the mind controlling the body, will help you be victorious over your old sin nature.

Think of Paul's formula like this: the Spirit needs to be strengthened, the mind needs to be strengthened, and the body needs to be weakened. In order to consider ourselves dead to sin and yield the members of our bodies as instruments of righteousness rather than instruments of wickedness, we must take control of our bodies. We must deny our old sin nature the things the old nature wants, because the old nature has died. There are things I am no longer permitted to do because my body does not belong to me but to Christ.

Jesus understood the temptation to give into the flesh when Satan tempted him in the wilderness. The very first thing Satan tempted Jesus to do was to give into His fleshly needs. He had been in the desert for forty days without food. Satan tempted Him by saying, "If you are the Son of God, tell these stones to become bread" (Matthew 4:3). Jesus conformed His own thinking to the way the Father thinks when He responded, "It is written: Man does not live on bread alone, but on every word that comes from the mouth of God" (Matthew 4:4).

Jesus did not give into Satan's temptation because He used the formula: spirit, soul, and body. The divine nature of God renewed His mind into thinking the way God thinks and exercised power over His body. He denied Himself the pleasure of bread to eat. Jesus understood that there is something better than bread to nourish our lives—the Word of God. Spirit, soul, and body is the correct formula for Christian living, but each one requires discipline. You must surrender to the Spirit's control, study the Word of God, and deny your flesh the things that will keep Christ from being the center of your life.

The Result of Discipline

Discipline that comes through consistent study of God's Word, faithful gathering with other believers for worship, and earnest prayer will help keep you fit for the race. Winning is the result of hours of practice that come from a disciplined life. Many a racecar driver has yet to win the Cup Championship because he has refused to practice certain disciplines in his life. There is nothing like winning the big race or the big game. In football, the big game is the Super Bowl. Not everyone agrees that the Super Bowl is the ultimate game. Duane Thomas was a running back for the Dallas Cowboys in the 1970s. During the 1971 season, Duane stopped speaking to the media. No matter how hard they tried to talk to him he refused to speak to anyone before or after a game. Then the Cowboys won the Super Bowl. In a post game interview, Duane Thomas was asked, "How does it feel to win the ultimate game?" Thomas replied, "If it is the ultimate game, then why do they play it every year?"

In baseball, the big game is the World Series. In basketball, the big game is the NBA Championship. In racing, the big race is Daytona. But even winning at Daytona cannot compare to winning the Cup Championship at the end of the season. Winning the cup is something every team begins the season wanting to accomplish. While there are accomplishments other than winning the Cup, the Cup is what every team works so hard to achieve.

"Everyone who competes in the games goes into strict training. They do it to get a crown that will not last; but we do it to get a crown that will last forever" (1 Corinthians 9:25). There is celebration in Victory Lane. That is where all the hard work and dedication to practice pays off. For the believer, the same could be said of standing before God one day. All the time spent in the study of God's Word, the times you denied yourself of earthly pleasures to do something for the Kingdom of God, will be worth the sacrifice when you hear Jesus' words, "Well done, thy good and faithful servant!"

There are many things that can disqualify a person from the race. Perhaps the most likely is a lack of discipline in your life. I would encourage you to take the advice of the apostle Paul in Romans, chapter 6. Begin by considering your old sin nature to be dead and by yielding your body as an instrument for God's service. Use the energy you once used to serve a life of sin to serve the Lord Jesus Christ. Make the effort to practice the Christian life. Each day determine to deny yourself the things that will harm your walk with God and cause someone else to stumble. Don't be disqualified because of the lack of discipline in your spiritual walk. Understand that everything may be permissible now that you are under grace and not law, but not everything is profitable. There are certain actions that will cost you more than you know.

Speeding on pit row can cost a team laps in a race, ultimately costing them points toward the Cup Championship. Many times this happens out of carelessness or because the driver is not paying attention. Pay attention to what is happening in your life. Make your body a servant rather than your master. By practicing self-discipline, you will be fit for the race, and you will enjoy a great celebration in heaven.

Debris in the Road

Matt Kenseth was down on all fours at the 2004 Indianapolis Speedway, peering underneath the right front fender of the DeWalt Ford, shaking his head in disbelief, when crew chief Robbie Reiser leaned down beside him. They'd rarely, if ever, seen such damage from a piece of debris.

"Seriously, I've never seen debris tear up a car like that," Rider said. "It knocked the sway bar tube and everything right off the car. It's major."

The debris in question appeared to be a piece of lead that was lying in turn four when Gordon and Kenseth coursed through the corner with some twenty laps remaining. Gordon struck the object, tearing a large chunk out of the right valance of his Chevrolet. Fortunately for Gordon, the eventual race winner, there wasn't more damage.

"It was significant, wasn't something small. It was really big," Gordon said. "All I could do was envision Martinsville, and how torn up that car was. We were fortunate. Matt was very unfortunate. I felt very bad for them and what they had to go through. I don't know how long it was there, don't even know what it was. But I do know that I looked in my mirror and that Kenseth certainly got the worst of it. I don't know how in the world that piece of debris flew underneath my racecar and got him the way it did, and didn't get us. But I was pretty animated that somebody should have recognized that."

Once the debris cleared Gordon's car, it hit Kenseth, effectively foiling a potential victory in one of NASCAR's most coveted races. He pitted, telling his team he thought a tire was going flat. As he exited the pits, NASCAR threw the caution flag. In the end, Kenseth finished 16th.

Just as there are many hazards in a road race, in the Christian life there are many obstacles. In the second half of this book, I have tried to address some of the things that can disqualify a believer from the race.

What does it mean to be disqualified? "No, I beat my body and make it my slave so that after I have preached to others, I myself will not be disqualified for the prize" (1 Corinthians 9:27). When the apostle Paul wrote about being disqualified, he did not imply that a believer can lose his or her salvation.

The word "disqualified" is translated from the Greek word "adokimos." It was used when ancient coins were melted down because they no longer had the weight of their numerical value. Currency was valued by weight as well as numeric value. Since currency was made of silver and gold, people would often shave off portions of the currency. After a while, by shaving just a little from a lot of coins, a person would have piles of silver and gold to be sold. The authorities would periodically weigh currency to make sure the numeric value equaled the weighted value. If the weighted value did not equal the numeric value, they would discard the coins and melt them. The discarded pile was labeled as "adokimos" or disapproved.

Paul was most likely referring to this when he used the term "adokimos" in 1 Corinthians 9:27. His fear for his Christian race was that God would measure his life and find him lacking. He was not concerned about losing his salvation as much as losing his influence. Many a man and woman of God have lost their influence for Jesus Christ due to an undisciplined area in their life. The Bible clearly teaches that once a person is truly saved they can never be lost. The weight of the evidence in the Bible is clear that God never disowns His people.

> My sheep listen to my voice; I know them, and they follow me. I give them eternal life, and they shall never perish; no one can snatch them out of my hand. My Father, who has given them to me, is greater than all; no one can snatch them out of my Father's hand. I and the Father are one.
> —John 10:27–30

> What, then, shall we say in response to this? If God is for us, who can be against us? He who did not spare his own Son, but gave him up for us all—how will he not also, along with him, graciously give us all things? Who will bring any charge against those whom God has chosen? It is God who justifies.

Who is he that condemns? Christ Jesus, who died—more than that, who was raised to life—is at the right hand of God and is also interceding for us. Who shall separate us from the love of Christ? Shall trouble or hardship or persecution or famine or nakedness or danger or sword? As it is written: "For your sake we face death all day long; we are considered as sheep to be slaughtered." No, in all these things we are more than conquerors through him who loved us. For I am convinced that neither death nor life, neither angels nor demons, neither the present nor the future, nor any powers, neither height nor depth, nor anything else in all creation, will be able to separate us from the love of God that is in Christ Jesus our Lord.

—Romans 8:31–39

Sin in your life will not cause God to disown you. Sin in your life *will* cause you to lose your influence with unbelievers. There are believers who once stood very strong for Jesus Christ. They did incredible things for the Lord. They served faithfully, but today they have fallen out of the race. They have allowed some debris in the road of life to distract them from what God purposed their life to accomplish. They have been put on a shelf as far as God is concerned. They no longer stand as a testimony of God's grace and power. Perhaps they were disqualified by money, material things, or uncontrolled lust, but the reality is that they are no longer contenders. They did not lose their salvation, but they lost their influence. The danger of debris in the road is that the debris can cause you to wreck, and by wrecking, you may cause others to wreck too. A blown tire in turn three can result in slamming into the wall, causing an uncontrollable automobile to ram into others, which results in their disqualification.

Our lives have influence. When we fall out of the race, we take others with us, like our spouse, our children, a co-worker, or a friend. Very few accidents affect only the person responsible. There are many reasons why the yellow caution flag comes out in a race, but the most common is debris on the track. Several things can cause debris, such as a fan tossing something onto the track, something falling off one of the cars, or the results of an accident. Whatever the reason, debris on the track is dangerous. Even the smallest item can cause disastrous results.

Satan is a master at tossing debris in the road of life. His most common debris is distraction. Satan wants to distract you from the race God has marked out for your life. He will attempt to distract you with earthly distractions. Jesus reminded us that His kingdom was not of this world. As citizens of His kingdom, our thoughts should be with Him. Jesus prayed these words the night before He died:

> I have revealed you to those whom you gave me out of the world. They were yours; you gave them to me and they have obeyed your word. Now they know that everything you have given me comes from you. For I gave them the words you gave me and they accepted them. They knew with certainty that I came from you, and they believed that you sent me. I pray for them. I am not praying for the world, but for those you have given me, for they are yours. All I have is yours, and all you have is mine. And glory has come to me through them. I will remain in the world no longer, but they are still in the world, and I am coming to you. Holy Father, protect them by the power of your name—the name you gave me—so that they may be one as we are one. While I was with them, I protected them and kept them safe by that name you gave me. None has been lost except the one doomed to destruction so that Scripture would be fulfilled. I am coming to you now, but I say these things while I am still in the world, so that they may have the full measure of my joy within them. I have given them your word and the world has hated them, for they are not of the world any more than I am of the world. My prayer is not that you take them out of the world but that you protect them from the evil one. They are not of the world, even as I am not of it. Sanctify them by the truth; your word is truth. As you sent me into the world, I have sent them into the world. For them I sanctify myself, that they too may be truly sanctified. My prayer is not for them alone. I pray also for those who will believe in me through their message, that all of them may be one, Father, just as you are in me and I am in you. May they also be in us so that the world may believe that you have sent me.
>
> —John 17:6–21

Jesus prayed for the apostles and for us. He says in verse twenty that He prayed for all who would believe in Him through the apostles' message. That means us. We are not of this world. Our thoughts and ideas are in heaven where Christ is preparing our eternal home. All we have known thus for is the life we have lived here on earth. Being distracted from heaven and what our lives were meant to accomplish is easy when you consider all that we have to do on earth. We have jobs and families to take care of. We have hobbies and responsibilities. As born-again believers, we must keep the main thing the main thing. The main thing for the believer is to keep our eyes and thoughts on heaven. As a racecar driver must keep his eyes on the road and his mind on the race, we must keep our eyes on heaven and our mind on the Lord Jesus Christ. The most effective way to deal with earthly distractions is to have a heavenly mind.

> Since, then, you have been raised with Christ, set your hearts on things above, where Christ is seated at the right hand of God. Set your minds on things above, not on earthly things. For you died, and your life is now hidden with Christ in God. When Christ, who is your life, appears, then you also will appear with him in glory. Put to death, therefore, whatever belongs to your earthly nature: sexual immorality, impurity, lust, evil desires and greed, which is idolatry. Because of these, the wrath of God is coming. You used to walk in these ways, in the life you once lived. But now you must rid yourselves of all such things as these: anger, rage, malice, slander, and filthy language from your lips. Do not lie to each other, since you have taken off your old self with its practices and have put on the new self, which is being renewed in knowledge in the image of its Creator.
> —Colossians 3:1–10

In order to have our minds on heaven, we need a heavenly vision, heavenly values, and heavenly virtues.

Heavenly Vision

It would be awesome to look into heaven right now—like the beloved disciple John did when he wrote the book of Revelation. What a blessing as God unveiled his eyes and allowed him to peek into heaven and see the streets of gold. Steven also had a heavenly vision when the Jews were stoning him. He saw Jesus standing beside the throne of God. The apostle Paul states in Colossians, chapter 3, that you and I can also have a heavenly vision. He invites us to set our minds and hearts on the things above, as opposed to earthly things. According to Paul, we have already been raised with Christ. When Christ arose from the dead, we arose with Him. Because Christ is now seated at the right hand of the Father, we are seated with Him.

There are only two types of people in the world. There are people in Christ, and there are people outside of Christ. God sent two men into this world without a sin nature, Adam and Christ. By virtue of natural birth, we are in Adam. Everyone can trace his or her heritage back to him. But Adam failed the test. He disobeyed God by eating the forbidden fruit, and he died. Everyone is born in Adam and suffers from the consequences of Adam's sin. God sent a second Adam into the world, Jesus Christ. He obeyed God and did not fail. In order to receive the benefits of His obedience, a person must be reborn. This is the result of faith. All mankind is either in Adam or in Christ. We are in Adam by natural birth and in Christ by spiritual birth. You can read more about this in Romans, chapter 5 and 1 Corinthians, chapter 15.

If you are in Christ, you receive the benefit of His obedience, which is eternal life in heaven. Being in Christ means He *is* our life. When you accept Christ as personal Savior, His life becomes your life. You not only become His, but also you exchange your life for His. Christ is our life, according to Colossians 3:4. That means when He came out of the grave, all believers arose with Him. When He ascended back to heaven, all believers ascended with Him. He is seated today at the right hand of the Father, and all believers are seated with Him.

Paul stated, "I have been crucified with Christ and I no longer live, but Christ lives in me. The life I live in the body, I live by faith in the Son of God, who loved me and gave himself for me" (Galatians 2:20).

Christ did more than give us life, He is our life. Christ can do anything through us. Our life is not about what *we* can do but what Christ can do *through* us. To have a heavenly vision is to see yourself as Christ sees you. You may see yourself as sinful and defeated by sinful thoughts and habits, but God sees you as He sees Jesus Christ—holy, blameless, righteous, and without sin. Our position is in Christ, and our potential is to be like Christ. Stop thinking of yourself as a defeated sinner and see yourself with all the potential God sees in you, because His Son lives in you and can do anything. The things of the world distract you when, in truth, the things in the world are not what you should be focused on. Your vision should be on the eternal and not the earthly.

Heavenly Values

There are two things to keep in mind if you expect to have heavenly values over earthly ones. First, you must think about the Lord, and second, you must love the Lord. After telling us to set our *hearts* on the things above, Paul writes that we must set our *minds* on things above in Colossians 3:2. God wants us to have heavenly thoughts. We should start thinking about the things of heaven. When was the last time you read Revelation 21–22? Those two chapters tell us about our eternal home. They describe the beauty and splendor of heaven. But there is more than the beauty of heaven to motivate us to think heavenly thoughts. There are relationships with saints, past and present, to motivate us. There is the eternal life of no separation and no pain to make us think about heaven. And there is the reality that we will fall at the feet of the one who made everything and join with the heavenly chorus declaring that He is worthy!

You can get so distracted by your problems and life issues that you forget they are temporal. The adversity and difficulty you may find yourself in today will soon be gone. There will be no problems in heaven. There will be no sickness and disease in heaven. There will be no bills to pay or death to separate us from loved ones in heaven. Hallelujah! Though the pain we experience from those things on earth is real, it is only temporary in the light of eternity. Material things are temporal; heavenly things are eternal.

"Therefore we do not lose heart. Though outwardly we are wasting away, yet inwardly we are being renewed day by day. For our light and momentary troubles are achieving for us an eternal glory that far outweighs them all. So we fix our eyes not on what is seen, but on what is unseen. For what is seen is temporary, but what is unseen is eternal" (2 Corinthians 4:16–18). Paul reminds us that while troubles and trials may seem like they will never end, they are light and momentary. They may not seem light and momentary at the time. You may think right now your pain and suffering will never go away, but it will. I have watched many people struggle at the end of their lives. The pain associated with their terminal disease has taken a toll on their physical bodies, and watching them suffer is painful. Your heart breaks for them and what they have been through, but just moments after their passing, you know their suffering is over. Their pain and light trouble has achieved a glory far outweighing their suffering.

The same is also true for the things we hold onto in this life. The things we hold dear and cherish as being of earthly value must not be the things we set our affection on. They, too, shall pass away. They are temporal and will not last. They are ours to enjoy for a time. We have them, but they will all be gone tomorrow. Heaven and Jesus will be ours for eternity. Fix your eyes on the unseen things today, because they are the things that last. Think about the Lord!

Loving the Lord is also important in order to have a heavenly value system. Jesus said, "For where your treasure is, there your heart will be also" (Matthew 6:21). I have come to understand that I need to love heaven more than I love the earth. When I read about heaven and long to be in heaven, earthly things are put in perspective. I enjoy my life on this earth. God has surrounded me with wonderful family and friends. He has blessed my life with more material possessions than I deserve, but I cannot allow these things to be a distraction from heavenly values. The things of heaven are more important than the things of earth. Helen H. Lemmel wrote, "Turn your eyes upon Jesus, look full in His wonderful face: and the things of earth will grow strangely dim, in the light of His glory and grace."

Heavenly Virtues

In Colossians 3, the apostle Paul states:

> Put to death, therefore, whatever belongs to your earthly nature: sexual immorality, impurity, lust, evil desires and

greed, which is idolatry. Because of these, the wrath of God is coming. You used to walk in these ways, in the life you once lived. But now you must rid yourselves of all such things as these: anger, rage, malice, slander, and filthy language from your lips. Do not lie to each other, since you have taken off your old self with its practices and have put on the new self, which is being renewed in knowledge in the image of its Creator. Here there is no Greek or Jew, circumcised or uncircumcised, barbarian, Scythian, slave or free, but Christ is all, and is in all. Therefore, as God's chosen people, holy and dearly loved, clothe yourselves with compassion, kindness, humility, gentleness and patience. Bear with each other and forgive whatever grievances you may have against one another. Forgive as the Lord forgave you. And over all these virtues put on love, which binds them all together in perfect unity.

—Colossians 3:5–12

In verses five through nine, Paul mentions several things that can distract a believer:

Sexual Immorality—Sexual sin can disqualify a person from the race faster than any other sin. It can get hold of your life and destroy you. It can destroy your family and will rob a person of his or her true identity as well as lead to more sin. David's sexual sin with Bathsheba later led to murder when he placed her husband on the front line of the battle with their enemy. The Bible's answer to sexual sin is to run. "Flee from sexual immorality" (1 Corinthians 6:18). The Bible instructs believers to resist the devil but to flee sexual sin. You can stand toe to toe against the devil, and you can resist him, but when sexual sin comes knocking, you'd better lace up your running shoes and sprint away.

Impurity—This word implies moral defilement. When people begin to loosen their morals, they are heading down a slippery slope. Loose morals will lead to loose behavior. When we loosen our morals, we begin allowing things into our lives that will distract us and may very well cost us our influence. Loose morals will lead a person to justify his or her actions by what others do rather than what God says.

Lust—Lust is the disgraceful use of passion. God created passion as a good thing between a husband and wife. There is nothing wrong with passion between spouses, but when passion is used in a disgraceful way it turns to lust. Lusting after anything is wrong. The lust for money can be as harmful as lust for another woman or man.

Evil Desires—There are evil people in the world who would rather do evil than good. They have no conscience about hurting someone or harming something.

Greed—Greed can destroy families. People can turn into monsters because of greed. Family members turn against one another over their share of an inheritance. The desire to have something without effort or sacrifice can distract people from what they were intended to do in life.

Anger—Many believers have allowed their anger to control their lives. Uncontrolled anger will disqualify you from the race. You may think your anger is justified, but if you do not control your anger, it *will* control you. When you are angry, you cannot think about anything else. The person you are angry with will dominate your life. When you are angry toward an individual, that person owns you, because you cannot get the person or what he or she did off your mind. Anger will surface at the oddest times. You may not be able to sleep, read, or pray because of your anger.

Rage—This is the desire to hurt back. Because you have been hurt, you have rage toward someone and you want to retaliate. Road rage leads people to do foolish things. They get out of their automobiles on a busy highway and shoot at people in another car, or they run people off the road because someone cut them off in traffic. Human nature may be to strike back at people who have hurt you, but Christ's nature would want you to forgive. Jesus said, "But I tell you who hear me: Love your enemies, do good to those who hate you, bless those who curse you, pray for those who mistreat you. If someone strikes you on one cheek, turn to him the other also. If someone takes your cloak, do not stop him from taking your tunic. Give to everyone who asks you, and if anyone takes what belongs to you, do not demand it back. Do to others as you would have them do to you" (Luke 6:27–31).

Malice—Malice is the attitude that wants to get even. There is a saying: "Don't hold a grudge, get even!" Jesus taught that we should repay evil with good. When you spend the time and energy to think of ways to get even with someone, you are wasting your time. Our time should be spent on things that bring peace and contentment to our lives, not on ways to even the score. You are distracted from the race when you are wasting time thinking of ways to get even.

Slander—Many times what we do not do with our lives we will do with our lips. We slander people with our words. Slander is worse than gossip: it's a deliberate attempt to harm or discredit someone. Human nature wants to lash out at the people who have hurt us. When someone says something about us, the natural response is to try and discredit him or her by slander. You may be perfectly right to defend yourself against what someone has said about you, but we are wrong when we attack others. The people who know you should not believe it, and the people who do not know you should not matter. We spend way too much time worrying about what people think about us rather than what God thinks about us.

Filthy language—Cursing should not come from the mouth of a believer. Jesus said, "But the things that come out of the mouth come from the heart, and these make a man 'unclean'" (Matthew 15:18). James wrote, "Can both fresh water and salt water flow from the same spring? My brothers, can a fig tree bear olives, or a grapevine bear figs? Neither can a salt spring produce fresh water" (James 3:11). Filthy language will cost you influence over those who do not know Jesus Christ.

Lying—Believers should tell the truth. Lying misrepresents the Lord Jesus Christ, who is Truth. When you lie, you have to remember what you said. My wonderful mother always told me that when you tell the truth you never have to remember what you said. Lying can distract you from the race, because when you start lying you will find yourself defending each lie with another lie.

As sure as there are some things to discard, there are some things to desire. In Colossians 3:11–12, the apostle Paul encourages us to add these things to our lives. His analogy is one of taking off old garments and putting on new ones. Take off the garments of lying, filthy language, and greed, and replace them with the garments of compassion, kindness, and humility. Just as the old will distract and disqualify you from the race, the new will keep you focused and fit for the race. These are the heavenly virtues we should strive for:

Compassion—This is the great motivator of service. Nothing motivates a person to help more than compassion. Jesus was moved with compassion for people. That is why He became involved in their lives. Every miracle recorded in the New Testament was motivated by compassion. For example, Jesus looked on the multitude following Him into the desert with compassion and was motivated to feed them. There were over 5,000 people with Him. Compassion will lead you to become involved in another person's life.

Kindness—Kindness goes a long way with people. We could certainly use a lot more of it in the world today. Jesus was kind. He did not need an invitation to help people. He saw human need, and He met human needs. Believers ought to be kind to one another. When was the last time you were kind to someone for no reason? When was the last time you opened the door for someone entering a building with you or picked up the phone to call someone just to let them know you were thinking about them? There are many ways to be kind.

Humility—"God opposes the proud but gives grace to the humble" (James 4:6). Humility represents heavenly virtues. God demonstrated true humility. "Your attitude should be the same as that of Christ Jesus: Who, being in very nature God, did not consider equality with God something to be grasped, but made himself nothing, taking the very nature of a servant, being made in human likeness. And being found in appearance as a man, he humbled himself and became obedient to death—even death on a cross!" (Philippians 2:5–8).

Gentleness—Gentleness respects people for who they are. We are all fearfully and wonderfully made according to the Bible. We should be gentle in how we deal with those God created. Jesus was gentle. He could have struck men with a curse for rejecting Him. He could have taken vengeance on those opposing Him, but He was gentle (Luke 23:34). Gentleness is a heavenly virtue to be put on.

Patience—This word means endurance. Jesus was a finisher. He completed the work He was sent to do. People who know Christ should know the importance of endurance. We do not have the luxury of quitting the race. All who have gone before us exhort us to finish and to finish well. We must be encouragers of men and women to remain patient in the race God has marked out for them.

Bearing with one Another—We are all different. We think differently, and we are not likely to agree on every single point. The attitude of heaven is to bear with people that look and act differently than you, as long as they know Christ. In a NASCAR race, there are maneuvers and moves unique to each driver. From week to week, there are things one driver does to the dismay of others, but they learn to get along. They learn to agree to disagree, and they bear with each other. The people of God must recognize this as a heavenly virtue.

Forgiveness—In my life, I have done things for which I have asked God's forgiveness. I have done things to others for which I have asked their forgiveness. To my knowledge, neither has ever failed to forgive me. I must also be forgiving. I cannot hold a grudge against a brother or sister in Christ. "For if you forgive men when they sin against you, your heavenly Father will also forgive you. But if you do not forgive men their sins, your Father will not forgive your sins" (Matthew 6:14–15). Enough said!

Love—The supreme heavenly virtue is love. Love is the greatest of all commandments and the essential one to being focused for the entire race. Satan will try to steal your affection for God with affection for something else. As I have written earlier, loving God the most is the challenge of the Christian life. There are things in our lives that steal our love for God. There are unresolved issues that happen among our brothers, sisters, and us. Those things distract us from loving people the way Christ wants us to love them. Satan is a master at throwing debris on the road of life to distract your love. Don't get distracted by the things that do not matter. "But seek first his kingdom and his righteousness, and all these things will be given to you as well" (Matthew 6:33).

We'll Do Better Next Week

10

On May 20, 2002, Casey Atwood, the rookie driver of the No. 19 Dodge Intrepid R/T, took Elliott's advice on succeeding at Martinsville, but he didn't get any breaks during the day. Atwood, who started 14th as the top qualifying rookie and the top Dodge, had a strong car and ran 10th for the early part of the race. Unfortunately, contact from behind from the No. 88 car in turn four spun him and left him stalled on the apron. Atwood rejoined the pack and remained two laps down for the day. NASCAR also held him in the pits during late caution for an unexpected pit lane infraction. He again returned to the field to make up spots, but he did not have enough laps left to gain positions. He finished the day at 24th.

"We didn't get a break today," Atwood said. "Everybody checked up off turn two. I got into the guy in front of me and Jarrett got into me and I got spun out. It was just hard luck. We had a good car. If we could have been up front all day, we could have made better pit calls and had better tires on the car all day. We had a top-ten car pretty easy, I believe. It didn't work out. Maybe we'll do better next time."

Perhaps you have heard the story about the little boy playing baseball. He was playing right field, and his father arrived a little late to the game. As he walked toward the field, the father noticed the score was already eighteen to nothing in favor of the other team. The game was still in the first inning. The man's son was yelling from right field at the batters on the other team, "Swing batter, batter swing!" In between his taunting of the other team, the little boy was encouraging his teammates. "Here we go guys! We will get this one out! Come on boys, let's get him!" The father of the little boy was surprised to see his son with such an upbeat, positive attitude. He didn't want to discourage his son, so he said hello as he walked by and asked, "What's the score, son?" The boy replied, "Eighteen to zero!" The father asked, "Well, son, why are you so excited?" The boy said, "Because we haven't been up to bat yet!" That is a great attitude to have during adversity.

One of the things I enjoy about sports is that there is always the next game. No matter what happens in the game today, there is always another game to be played. If you lose this week, there is always hope you can win next week. If you did awful in the game today, you can try to do better in the game next time. "We will do better next week," the coach reminds his players. The same is true for the NASCAR Cup Teams. One week a driver wrecks the car in turn two, he blows an engine in turn three, or he has a flat tire in turn one. Maybe the crew makes a costly mistake, or the driver is penalized for speeding in pit row. There is always next week, and each team enters with the same chances to win. The post race interviews are often similar with those disqualified from a race: "We'll do better next week. We'll go back to the garage, work on the car, move on to the next race, and we will do better."

That is also true in the Christian race. January 1st is one of our favorite days, because January 1st stands for new beginnings. January 1st begins like every other day, but usually takes on new meaning because the day begins a new year and usually represents new starts. "This is the year I will do better. This is the year I will finally change my life." These are just a couple of the many comments people make on New Year's Day. We hate Mondays because we have to go to work or school, but Monday is the beginning of a new week, and often that means a new start. Everyone likes to have a fresh start. In the Christian life, we get to have a new start. God is the God of new beginnings. Our faith in Jesus Christ allows us to start over.

Many people struggle with their past. Even born-again believers can be defeated by it. God has made it possible for you to deal with your past and to move on. He has an answer for your past.

> As for you, you were dead in your transgressions and sins, in which you used to live when you followed the ways of this world and of the ruler of the kingdom of the air, the spirit who is now at work in those who are disobedient. All of us also lived among them at one time, gratifying the cravings of our sinful nature and following its desires and

thoughts. Like the rest, we were by nature objects of wrath. But because of his great love for us, God, who is rich in mercy, made us alive with Christ even when we were dead in transgressions—it is by grace you have been saved. And God raised us up with Christ and seated us with him in the heavenly realms in Christ Jesus, in order that in the coming ages he might show the incomparable riches of his grace, expressed in his kindness to us in Christ Jesus. For it is by grace you have been saved, through faith—and this not from yourselves, it is the gift of God—not by works, so that no one can boast. For we are God's workmanship, created in Christ Jesus to do good works, which God prepared in advance for us to do.

—Ephesians 2:1–10

The Results of our Past

Before our accepting Christ as our personal Savior, Paul paints a pretty bleak picture of us. In Ephesians 2:1–3, Paul wrote three things about our past: we were dead; we were deceived; and we were defeated.

"You were dead in your transgressions and sins" (verse 1). He uses two words to define our wrongdoing—transgressions and sins. The word translated as "transgressions" comes from the Greek word "paraptoma-sin," meaning to step over the line. The idea is that God has drawn a line in the sand. We must not step over that line. However, we choose to step over the line anyway. We make a conscious decision to disobey what God has said.

The word translated as "sin" comes from the Greek word "hamartiais" meaning to *miss the mark*. "For all have sinned and fall short of the glory of God" (Romans 3:23). To fall short means to miss the target. The idea behind this word is that the person shoots an arrow toward a target, but the arrow falls short of the "bull's eye." The arrow does not go wide left or wide right of the target; it just falls short.

God has a target. His goal for everyone is perfection. As far as God is concerned, you and I did not even reach the target of righteousness. We fell *way* short of God's target. When Paul wrote that we were once dead in transgressions and sins, he implied that we were dead to spiritual things. The problem for unbelievers is they do not even know their condition. Those outside of Jesus Christ do not even know they are spiritually dead. They may think they have life and everything is fine, but they are separated from God because they have not believed in God's Son, Jesus Christ. That was our condition before we accepted Jesus Christ by faith. Our past was the same. We were dead in our transgressions and sins. We willingly stepped over the line of God's law, and we came well short of the goal God had in mind when He created us.

"You followed the ways of this world" (verse 2). Many people today are deceived into thinking that all is well when all is not well. Satan has led them to believe that they can go any way they choose. As long as they do not hurt anyone or as long as their good outweighs their bad, they will end up in heaven. "The god of this age has blinded the minds of unbelievers, so that they cannot see the light of the gospel of the glory of Christ, who is the image of God" (2 Corinthians 4:4).

Satan will do anything to keep people from knowing the truth about their sin. He blinds minds and deceives people. He uses religion and false teaching to deceive. The next chapter of this book addresses the subject of false teaching and how Satan masterfully uses false teaching to deceive people from putting their trust in Christ for the forgiveness of sins. Jesus Christ is the only antidote for our sin, but Satan does not want you to know that. He wants you to think you can get to heaven other ways. You can follow the crowd. The way leading to death is a broad and crowded way, according to Jesus. The majority are going this way. Many go through the gate leading to death because Satan has deceived them into thinking his way is acceptable. "Enter through the narrow gate. For wide is the gate and broad is the road that leads to destruction, and many enter through it. But small is the gate and narrow the road that leads to life, and only a few find it" (Matthew 7:13).

We once followed the ways of the world. We were deceived into thinking everything was fine. We believed we could do anything we wanted to do, and as long as no one was hurt, we would be fine. But now we know differently. The light of the gospel of Jesus Christ has illuminated our lives and revealed Jesus Christ as the only way to heaven. God's light has shown us that while certain behaviors may be acceptable in some circles, they are not acceptable for followers of Jesus Christ. We are deceived only because we choose to ignore the internal witness of the Holy Spirit who guides us to all truth. You cannot do much about past deception, but you do not have to remain deceived.

"Gratifying the cravings of our sinful nature and following its desires and thoughts" (verse 3). Before accepting Christ, our agenda revolved around ourselves. That is not the life of victory God promised. God created us to be overcomers and not underachievers. Before we met Christ, we had little power to change. We were defeated by the sin nature and were taught we had to change on our own. Part of Satan's deception is to make us think we could never be good enough or never do enough to earn God's favor. Many today struggle with their past, because their past is a constant reminder to them of their defeat. They tried to do better, but they failed, and Satan has convinced them they would fail again if they tried.

A certain man went into business with another man. The business partner convinced the man that if he would only invest a small amount of money, in no time, he would triple his investment. The man invested and did not ask any questions. True to his word, the business partner returned to the man with triple his money in a short time. After a few weeks, he came to the man asking for an investment again, but this time he asked for a much larger sum of money. He told him that what he had done before was illegal, and if the man refused to invest with him this time, the business partner would turn him into the authorities. He blackmailed the man into doing more the second time than he did the first time.

Satan uses our past as blackmail. He wants to convince us that because we have failed in the past, we will fail in the future. He convinces us that we cannot measure up to God's favor, and it is useless to try. When we try to do better or take a step to improve our lives, Satan will remind us of what we did in the past and deceive us into thinking we cannot please God no matter how hard we try. This is so unfortunate, because God does not wait for us to get better before He loves us. He loved us when we were His enemies. "Very rarely will anyone die for a righteous man, though for a good man someone might possibly dare to die. But God demonstrates his own love for us in this: While we were still sinners, Christ died for us" (Romans 5:7–8).

Do not wait until you get better to come to Jesus Christ. Come to Christ the way you are, and He will make you everything He wants you to be. He will never love you less, because He could never love you any more than He loved you when He gave His life for you on the cross.

One little boy said he asked Jesus how much He loved him, and Jesus stretched out His arms and died for him. That is how much He loves you too. He can make you better. He can help you gain victory over the cravings of your sinful desires, and He can help you so you no longer follow the desires and thoughts of your sin nature. Your past may have been dead, deceived, and defeated, but with Christ you can have a new start!

The Remedy for our Past

A personal relationship with Jesus Christ is the remedy for our past. Paul writes, "For it is by grace you have been saved, through faith" (Ephesians 2:8). God's remedy for our past is to forgive, free, and fill us.

The most effective way to deal with someone who has done you wrong is to forgive him or her. That is what God did for us. Our sins nailed Jesus Christ to the cross. People have wondered for centuries: Who is responsible for Christ's death? Were the Jews? Were the Romans? Were the religious leaders at fault? Did the Roman soldiers kill Jesus? The truth is that our sins crucified Jesus Christ. He died in our place. "He himself bore our sins in his body on the tree, so that we might die to sins and live for righteousness; by his wounds you have been healed" (1 Peter 2:24).

We crucified the Son of God, but He chose to forgive us for what we did. God's answer for your past is forgiveness. He takes our sins and casts them into the sea of His forgetfulness and does not hold them over us. He does not blackmail us the way Satan does. He forgives us so we can be free from our past and free to serve Him in the future. This ought to be the way you forgive those who have hurt you. Forgiveness means to treat the person like he or she never did anything wrong. That is how God treats us. He does not remember our sin. He forgives and He forgets our sins. What about you? Are you holding a grudge against someone for something that happened in the past? Choose to forgive that person and move on. Do not allow the grudge you hold over something that happened so long ago keep you from experiencing God's peace in your life.

"For we are God's workmanship, created in Christ Jesus to do good works, which God prepared in advance for us to do" (verse 10). God forgives us in order that He can free us to serve Him. While Israel was in Egypt, the people were not free to serve God. They were in bondage to the Egyptians and were not allowed to serve their God as He deserved. The Egyptian Pharaoh was in charge of their comings and goings. But when they were redeemed from Egypt by the blood of the Passover lamb, they were set free. They were free to worship when and how they wanted. They were free to make sacrifices to their God and to worship at His altar. They built the Tabernacle, and they sang praises to Yahweh.

There is no greater comparison to the bondage of sin than the history of Israel in Egypt. Our Heavenly Father has redeemed us from our sin by the Passover Lamb, Jesus Christ, so we can do good works. Good works do not save us, but they declare our salvation to be genuine. When Christ moves into our lives, He brings the power to change and to overcome our past. Faith that does not have accompanying works is not genuine faith. "Faith by itself, if it is not accompanied by action, is dead" (James 2:17).

We were created to do good works, according to Ephesians 2:10. Good works for God are difficult when you are in bondage to sin. Sin will steal your ability to serve God. Sin takes over your life, and you become enslaved to the pleasures and desires of sin. In order to help us leave the past in the past, God removes our past. When people say we are saved and kept by grace, they do not mean we are free to do anything we choose. They mean we are free to serve God the way we should, because we are no longer under the grip of our past sins. God's remedy for what we have done in the past is to wipe our slate clean.

"And you, being dead through your transgressions and the uncircumcision of your flesh, you, [I say], did he make alive together with him, having forgiven us all our transgressions; having blotted out the bond written in ordinances that was against us, which was contrary to us: and he hath taken it out that way, nailing it to the cross" (Colossians 2:13–14, ASV). To blot out means to wipe clean. God wiped the slate clean for us with the blood of Jesus Christ. He wiped the slate clean so we could have a fresh start. And He keeps wiping the slate clean when we confess our sins. "If we confess our sins, he is faithful and just and will forgive us our sins and purify us from all unrighteousness" (1 John 1:9).

God forgives our sins in order that we can be free to serve Him and not be haunted by our past. He does more. God fills us with the Holy Spirit. The Holy Spirit is God's agent of change in our lives. He helps us to do better next time. The reason our past should not hinder our present and future is that God has replaced our past, sinful nature with His divine nature. Once we were dead in transgressions and sins, but now we are alive through His holy nature living inside of us. On our own, we are not any more capable of doing good works and living for God than we were before. The difference is that the Holy Spirit lives in us now. He enables us to do what God desires from us. As long as Christ is in us, He will forgive us, because He cannot occupy a sinful house. Since Christ will never leave us or forsake us, we understand He will always forgive us.

When I was a young boy, I enjoyed playing sports. If you could bounce it, kick it, throw it, or hit it, I liked it. I played every sport, and I would spend hours in the backyard pretending. There were many Super Bowl and World Series games played in my backyard. Many times I would envision myself throwing the winning touchdown pass or pitching the final strikeout. I always wanted those plays to be perfect, and so I would execute the play. If it was not just perfect, I would say, "Do over!"

God allows us to do things over that we may have failed to do correctly before. His answer for your past failure is to give you new opportunities to succeed.

Maybe you feel as if you've failed in your past. Maybe you have "blown it" in life. Even as a Christian, you may have failed to be faithful to God. You wonder if there is any hope. Satan has convinced you that you are unfit for the race, and you are close to giving up. Don't be a victim of your past! You can start over right now. Ask God to forgive you for your past. Accept His word that He will forgive you when you agree with Him regarding your sin. Most importantly, move on.

I have been on many diets in my life. Like most Americans, I struggle trying to maintain the proper weight. Experts tell us that a proper diet and faithful exercise is the best way to live healthy. As much as we try, we often fail. Where we fail the most is by not getting back on track. We allow our failure one day to turn into a week and then a month. Before we know it, we've been off our diet and exercise for a long time. Experts tell us that if we fail one day, then we must start right back the next day. Get back to doing the right thing.

I would encourage you, if you have fallen victim to some past sin in your life, you have a loving Savior who wants to forgive and restore you. Satan's lie is that you cannot do better. You *can* do better, and with God's grace, you will.

Next week's race is what motivates the people in NASCAR to keep going when they have been disqualified from earlier races. They get the chance to do it all again. Get back into the race. There is a new race starting right now. You have just as much potential to finish well as anyone. What are you waiting for?

You Need to Know the Rules

O n October 6, 2005, NASCAR announced that three Cup Series crew chiefs had been suspended, fined, and placed on probation due to rules violations stemming from the October 1, 2005, race at Talladega Super speedway.

Rules are everywhere. There are rules for almost everything we do in life. Our favorite board games have rules. Sporting events are played by rules, and NASCAR races have rules. There are rules for the track, the car, and caution flags, as well as rules for the drivers and crewmembers. Everyone benefits from knowing the rules. Failure to know the rules can lead to disqualification.

The Christian life is no different. If you want to be successful in the race, you must be familiar with the rules. The rules are the doctrines of the faith and not a list of do's and don'ts. The Christian life is not about rules. Jesus Christ set us free from a life of rules. The Pharisees were legalists in the first century. Their idea of religion was to live according to the law. They were more interested in people doing things right than they were in people doing the right things. Jesus' message was that God is more interested in the heart than outward performance. Jesus taught that true religion begins on the inside and works out. Many today want to start with the outside, and they think that by changing the outward appearance, people will change on the inside. Socialism promises to put new suits on every man, whereas Christianity wants to put new men in every suit.

Jesus taught us to love God with our whole heart and soul. The people who love God with their entire hearts and souls will not need a list of rules to live their lives. When we love God with our whole heart and soul, we want to do things that please the Lord. Loving God with our whole heart will help us to avoid things that displease our God. With the Holy Spirit as our guide and conscience, we do not need a list of rules or laws. He convicts and convinces us when our ways are not pleasing to the Father.

The rules addressed in this chapter are much like the rules in a NASCAR event. They are the things that will disqualify a person because he or she ignored them and tried to live life the way he or she pleased, rather than according to the standard God has set for us in the Bible. I am talking about the basic Bible doctrines that are important to how we run the race. False doctrine can be the most dangerous weapon Satan uses to disqualify people from the race. He is a master of deception. He prides himself on deceiving people into believing a lie over truth. Satan counterfeits God's truth with lies to lead people away from God, usually with just enough truth to trap them. You need to familiarize yourself with God's truth, so you will be ready when Satan tries to deceive.

Satan has deceived many people. Some were just like you. They started out in the Christian race. They may have grown up attending a Bible-believing church. They may have been taught the stories of the Bible in Sunday school classes. Today they have been led away from God by false teaching or by no teaching at all. Even though we are on a mission to evangelize the unbelievers, we realize that there are many believers struggling today to remain faithful to the truth. Some have been deceived and are no longer active in the race. They were disqualified because they fell victim to Satan's deception. Breaking the rules of NASCAR will disqualify a racecar driver faster than any other thing. NASCAR teams study the rules so they will not violate them.

The more you study Bible doctrine, the less likely it is that you will be defeated by Satan's deception. As sure as there is a devil, you can be certain that he will try to deceive you in order to disqualify you from the race. The Bible declares Satan to be the father of all lies (John 8:44). Satan tried to deceive the Son of God. We can be sure he will try to deceive believers today. The apostle Paul wrote these words to his young friend Timothy:

> The Spirit clearly says that in later times some will abandon the faith and follow deceiving spirits and things taught by demons. Such teachings come through hypocritical liars,

whose consciences have been seared as with a hot iron. They forbid people to marry and order them to abstain from certain foods, which God created to be received with thanksgiving by those who believe and who know the truth. For everything God created is good, and nothing is to be rejected if it is received with thanksgiving, because it is consecrated by the word of God and prayer. If you point these things out to the brothers, you will be a good minister of Christ Jesus, brought up in the truths of the faith and of the good teaching that you have followed. Have nothing to do with godless myths and old wives' tales; rather, train yourself to be godly. For physical training is of some value, but godliness has value for all things, holding promise for both the present life and the life to come. This is a trustworthy saying that deserves full acceptance (and for this we labor and strive), that we have put our hope in the living God, who is the Savior of all men, and especially of those who believe.

—1 Timothy 4:1–10

There are many religions in the world. Some believe there are different ways to go to heaven. They think what a person believes does not really matter as long as that person is sincere. People can be sincerely wrong. Those who do not believe that Jesus Christ is the only way to heaven are misguided. People have the right to believe any way they choose, but they may not go to heaven. Jesus taught that a very narrow way leads to life, and He is the way. The reason I accept His words over the views of others is that He arose from the dead. You can go to the graves of other religious leaders today, and their graves are marked. Here lies . . . .

When you go to the tomb where Jesus was laid, you will not find Him. He is not in the grave because He arose from the dead. When Jesus arose from the dead, He validated everything He ever said. His resurrection gave proof to His claims, because that was His most powerful statement. Jesus said He would rise from the dead. All the other religious icons are dead. Jesus is alive! His resurrection was powerful, but more importantly, by rising from the dead, He gave power to the words He spoke. His resurrection made His words credible.

Departure from the Truth

The apostle Paul told Timothy that false teaching would arise in the church. He forecasted to his young friend that people would abandon the faith and follow deceiving spirits. That was not the only time Paul warned of false teachers. Timothy was located in the city of Ephesus when Paul wrote the book of 1 Timothy. In Acts, chapter 20, the apostle Paul met the Elders of the church in Ephesus and spoke these words: "I know that after I leave, savage wolves will come in among you and will not spare the flock. Even from your own number men will arise and distort the truth in order to draw away disciples after them. So be on your guard!" (Acts 20:29–31a).

The antidote to false teaching is solid teaching. Paul encourages Timothy to teach truth. Truth is the best way people will be able to identify false teachings. You do not have to study the occult in order to identify their false teachings. If you saturate your mind with God's truth, you will be able to identify false teaching when you hear it. All false teaching comes from the same source. False teaching comes from deceiving spirits and demons, according to 1 Timothy 2:1.

There is really nothing new under the sun. All false teaching can be traced to the same lie started in the Garden of Eden. Satan deceived Eve into thinking that if she ate the forbidden fruit then she could become like God. Satan convinced Eve that God was holding something really good back from her. He told her that if God really did love her, He would allow her to eat from the Tree of Knowledge of Good and Evil (Genesis 3:4–5). That same lie used on Eve was the one he tried on Jesus. This is the same lie Satan uses on us. Satan wants us to think that God does not really love us.

When Satan tried to deceive Jesus with lies, Jesus defeated Satan with Scripture. Jesus knew the rules. Satan offered Jesus three tests. First, he tempted Jesus to satisfy his hunger by commanding the stones be made into bread. If He was hungry, and since He had the power to do it, Jesus should turn the stones into bread and satisfy His hunger. Jesus' answer was "man does not live by bread alone" (Matthew 4:4).

Secondly, he invited Jesus up to the highest point on the Temple and used some Scripture of his own. He quoted from Psalm 91 and asked Jesus to prove that He was the Son of God by throwing Himself over and letting God send His angels to protect Him. That is what Satan does. He wants to distort truth by manipulating Scripture. Satan takes things out of context. That is why Jesus said to Satan in Matthew 4:7, "It is *also* written!" "It is *also* written, do not put the Lord your God to the test." Jesus demonstrated the importance of knowing all the rules. People make a big mistake when they build doctrine around one verse and do not consider the entire Bible. That is what Jesus meant when He said, "It is *also* written." Satan quoted a verse from the Bible, but he took that verse out of context.

Thirdly, Satan took Jesus up to a mountain and showed Him the sights (Matthew 4:8–9). He invited Jesus to bow down and worship him. If Jesus would bow to Satan, then Satan would give Jesus everything He saw. The only problem with that statement was that "everything He saw" wasn't Satan's to give. Jesus would gain the world, but it would come at the expense of the cross. Satan was trying to convince Jesus to bypass the cross and get His kingdom the easy way.

When the Bible says that Jesus was tempted in all the ways we are tempted (Hebrews 4:15), the Bible means that Jesus was tempted in three areas—the lust of the flesh, the lust of the eyes, and the pride of life. The first temptation to turn the stones into bread was Satan's way of trying to appeal to Jesus' flesh. Satan says, "If you are hungry, feed yourself." Satisfy your need. You and I face this same temptation today when Satan tells us to satisfy our needs at any cost. If you want it, then get it! Have it your way! This one is for you! Go for it! Grab the gusto! All of these are attempts to get people to satisfy their lust of the flesh.

The second temptation to bow down to Satan was his attempt to appeal to Jesus' lust of the eyes. The temptation is to "get it the easy way." See it and take it! The kingdom would come to Jesus, but after the cross. Before the victory comes the defeat. Before He would reign, He must suffer. Satan tempted Jesus to bypass the cross. Take it Satan's way. We need to realize our success and achievements come at a price. If a man does not work, he should not eat, the Bible says. Satan offers us pleasure and wants us to think we do not need to suffer. The idea of suffering and sacrifice are foreign to Satan.

The third temptation, when Satan asked Jesus to throw Himself off the Temple and prove He was God, was a temptation for Jesus' pride.

Satan invited Him to prove He was the Son of God. That temptation Jesus would encounter again at the cross, when the crowd called for Him to come down and prove His deity (Matthew 27:40). Satan tells us that we have to exercise our pride in life by demanding our rights and insisting on our own way. Pride has been the downfall of many. Satan's pride caused him to be cast from heaven in the first place. No wonder he tries to use pride to disqualify believers today.

"How you have fallen from heaven, O morning star, son of the dawn! You have been cast down to earth, you who once laid low the nations! You said in your heart, 'I will ascend to heaven; I will raise my throne above the stars of God; I will sit enthroned on the mount of assembly, on the utmost heights of the sacred mountain. I will ascend above the tops of the clouds; I will make myself like the Most High'" (Isaiah 14:12–13).

Jesus defeated each temptation and demonstrated the importance of knowing God's Word. God's Word is our weapon to defeat Satan's deception. You have to know and study God's Word so you can combat Satan's temptation with the right verse for the right battle. Jesus used the right verse for the right temptation. The words He used sent Satan packing.

Disregard for the Truth

The apostle Paul mentions several perversions of truth that occurred in the city of Ephesus. People were told not to marry. Others were told what kind of food to eat and not eat. The false teaching implied by these verses is not worth taking time to consider. False teaching changes with culture and time. The rules people teach we should live by today in America are different from the ones emphasized by people of different cultures and time periods. The important issue is that these things were not documented by God's truth. When a person begins to follow a false teaching or a false teacher, he or she falls victim to wrong conduct. When people reject truth, their imaginations take over. They begin to follow extremes. Many times people who drift from truth resort to a life of rules and regulations rather than pursuing a healthy relationship with Jesus Christ. They concern themselves with actions more than attitudes. They are more concerned that they look a certain way or act in a certain manner than with the condition of their hearts. They have disregarded the truth for corruption of truth. They substitute rules for relationships.

Some believers think doctrine does not matter. They do not think that knowing Bible doctrine is necessary. They believe that doctrine divides when, in fact, the understanding of Bible doctrine will protect you from deception. Satan has been revealed in the Bible as "an angel of light" (2 Corinthians 11:14). He will do anything to deceive us. As "a roaring lion," he often preys on our weakness (1 Peter 5:8). Satan may not be able to disqualify you by immorality or through some stronghold in your life, but he can deceive you with false teaching because you are not grounded in God's Word. You have not taken the time to understand God's Word. Satan will mix a little truth in the deception to get your attention and then lead you astray with an all-out perversion of the truth.

Defense of the Truth

> Command and teach these things. Don't let anyone look down on you because you are young, but set an example for the believers in speech, in life, in love, in faith and in purity. Until I come, devote yourself to the public reading of Scripture, to preaching and to teaching. Do not neglect your gift, which was given you through a prophetic message when the body of elders laid their hands on you. Be diligent in these matters; give yourself wholly to them, so that everyone may see your progress. Watch your life and doctrine closely. Persevere in them, because if you do, you will save both yourself and your hearers.
>
> —1 Timothy 4:11–16

If someone can talk you into something, then the chances are that someone else can talk you out of the same thing. We must learn to settle truth in our hearts and not be led astray by persuasive words. Paul exhorted Timothy to do five things: teach truth, set an example of truth, study truth, meditate on truth, and practice truth.

Teach the Truth—Jesus is truth. The best way to learn truth is to teach truth to others. Timothy would grow in truth as he studied God's truth in order to teach truth to others. You may not have the gift of teaching. You may never be called upon to teach a Bible study in church, but you can teach truth. There are people God has placed in your life to influence. Maybe they are your children, grandchildren, or just friends. They could be a spouse or a co-worker. Teach them the truth. When you verbalize truth, you will be reinforcing truth in your own life. As a pastor, I have the opportunity to teach people God's truth weekly. I must say that I get more out of preparing messages than the people probably get from hearing these messages.

Be an Example of the Truth—People practice what they really believe. Everything else is religious talk. If you really believe something to be true, you will practice it in your life. Your doctrine will determine your behavior. For this reason, we must live what we believe. People are more likely to believe a sermon they *see* than the ones they only *hear*.

Study the Truth—Nothing can replace study. You do not have to go to Seminary to study the Bible. Many resources are available today to help you study the Bible. Dig into God's Word and learn for yourself the things that will guard your soul from Satan's deception. Ignorance will not be a good excuse before your Maker one day. You cannot expect to tell God that you did not know. God expects us to know. He has written and preserved His Word for us to know. He has given us His Holy Spirit as a teacher and guide to help us understand truth.

Meditate on the Truth—Go over truth as often as possible. Take ownership of truth. Until you make the doctrines of the Bible your own, they will not be produced in your life. You must embrace God's truth as the standard for your life and settle for nothing less than God's best. Joshua understood the importance of meditating on God's Word: "Do not let this Book of the Law depart from your mouth; meditate on it day and night, so that you may be careful to do everything written in it. Then you will be prosperous and successful" (Joshua 1:8).

Practice the Truth—Remember the saying, "practice makes perfect." Live according to the things you believe. They will become normal behavior after awhile. A NASCAR driver does not have to think about the rules of racing because after awhile they become second nature to him. So will the basic doctrines of the faith, if you commit to putting them into practice.

The rules of the game are important. You do not get to make up the rules as you go. God has made the rules for the race, and He expects us to obey His rules. The most important rule is to believe that Jesus Christ has come in the flesh, and He died on the cross for your sins. Satan will mislead you and try to tell you Jesus was a mere man. He will tell you that Christ's death on the cross was unnecessary. The Bible declares that Christ's death was necessary. Christ's death was the only possible way for a sinful man to have a relationship with Holy God.

"Who is the liar? It is the man who denies that Jesus is the Christ. Such a man is the antichrist—he denies the Father and the Son" (1 John 2:22). Satan's goal is to deny the importance of the work Jesus did for you on the cross. He will do everything he can to cast doubt in your mind about the cross being necessary. He did everything in his power to keep Jesus from going to the cross. Praise God he failed to detour Jesus from going to the cross. I encourage you to be like Jesus. When He was confronted with Satan, Jesus knew the rules and defeated Satan at his own game by quoting Scripture. There is extreme power in the Word of God. Know the Word! Teach the Word! Meditate on His Word! Practice the Word, and be an example of His Word! This will keep you in the race and will certainly help you to finish the race well.

Conclusion 12

In the first half of this book, I tried to point out the parallels between what happens in pit row in a car race and what needs to happen in the life of a believer in order to run the Christian race. In chapter one, I compared the Word of God to our fuel for the race. A car requires fuel to operate, and the believer requires the Word of God. If you try to operate on anything besides God's Word, you are most likely to run out of fuel. God's Word is the only lasting fuel for the Christian life.

In chapter two, I compared worship to changing four tires on the racecar. Racecars need fresh tires in order to run faster and with greater stability on the track. Fresh tires provide balance for the road. We receive proper balance for the Christian race through worship. We were created to worship, and worshipping our God helps to bring balance to our lives.

In chapter three, I compared fellowship to changing the battery. When believers enjoy fellowship with other believers, they are encouraged. Encouragement helps us to continue the race. Our batteries sometimes lose power and need a boost. We receive a boost by meeting together with other believers and enjoying healthy Christian fellowship.

In chapter four, I compared prayer to talking with the crew chief on a Cup Team. The chief assimilates all the information that is given to him by the team and relays to the driver instructions for the race. Prayer is the line of communication God has opened with the believer to communicate with him or her.

In chapter five, I compared accountability to listening to your spotter. Spotters help the driver see things on the road that are invisible to the driver. The spotter communicates possible problems ahead and assists the driver through adverse conditions. God places people in our lives to help with our "blind spots." Everyone has "blind spots," and we can benefit from those who hold us accountable.

In chapter six, I mentioned that drivers require help during the race as much as the car does. Racecar drivers are given cold drinks to help them remain hydrated. A cold drink on a hot day can be very refreshing. You and I need to be refreshed in the Christian race. Our refreshment comes through the encouraging words we receive from other believers. Just as we need to be refreshed from time to time, we also need to provide encouraging words to others. There may very well be someone near you today who is in need of an encouraging word.

The second half of this book addressed the many pitfalls Satan places in our path in order to disqualify us from the race. Disqualification does not imply that we will not go to heaven, but that we can lose our influence over others. If Satan can distract us from serving God by casting doubt in our minds about God, we will lose our influence. Once a person is born again, he or she cannot lose salvation, but he or she can lose influence in the lives of others. Satan considers disqualifying us as much of a victory as blinding the mind of an unbeliever. The next best thing to deceiving unbelievers for Satan is disqualifying believers.

In chapter seven, I wrote about the importance of staying fit. Spiritual disciplines are required for the child of God to remain fit for the Christian race. Our bodies are the Temple of the Holy Spirit and are to be used as instruments of God's service. We need to bear in mind that in everything we do and everywhere we go, we involve the Lord Jesus Christ. He is our companion in life. He deserves to live in a clean house.

Two college roommates were talking one day. One said to the other, "I am thinking about getting a goat to live in our dorm room." The other student said, "What about the smell?" The roommate replied, "I think the goat will get used to it." The goat may not have minded living in a dirty room, but Christ deserves better.

Chapter eight was about practice. As we implement Paul's formula of Spirit, Soul, and Body, we can execute the right maneuvers in order to run the race that God has marked out for us.

Chapter nine was about the dreaded debris Satan throws in the road to cause accidents. Satan wants to blowout your tires or cause you to wreck in order to make others wreck. He uses every available debris he can find to cast doubt into our minds about God's love. We must concentrate on God's Word and learn from the example of Jesus, who defeated every temptation with Scripture.

Chapter ten reminded us that we can have a fresh start in Jesus Christ. While our old nature is at times overtaken in sin, we can confess our sins and find God faithful and just to forgive our sins and give us a fresh start. When we agree with God about our sin, He casts our sins as far as the east is from the west and remembers them no more.

I hope this book has been your inspiration to start over. Get back in the race today, and find yourself a good pit crew to help you get to Victory Lane.

But remember chapter eleven. What Satan may not be able to do with debris or doubt, he will try to do with false teaching. Do not be discouraged because you failed to familiarize yourself with God's truth. Stay in the Word of God. The Bible is not just the fuel to keep us running the race; the Bible is the rulebook that helps us celebrate in Victory Lane.